Abraham,
the Friend of God

Biblical figures 1

Abraham,
the Friend of God

Dr. Jaerock Lee

Abraham, the Friend of God by Dr. Jaerock Lee
Published by Urim Books (Representative: Sungnam Vin)
73, Yeouidaebang-ro 22-gil, Dongjak-Gu, Seoul, Korea
www.urimbooks.com

All rights reserved. This book or parts thereof may not be reproduced in any form, stored in a retrieval system, or transmitted in any form or by any means, electronic, mechanical, photocopying, recording or otherwise, without prior written permission of the publisher.

Unless otherwise noted, all Scripture quotations are taken from the Holy Bible, NEW AMERICAN STANDARD BIBLE, ®, Copyright © 1960, 1962, 1963, 1968, 1971, 1972, 1973, 1975, 1977, 1995 by The Lockman Foundation. Used by permission.

Copyright © 2019 by Dr. Jaerock Lee
ISBN: 979-11-263-0490-5 04230
ISBN: 979-11-263-0412-7 (set)
Translation Copyright © 2016 by Dr. Esther K. Chung. Used by permission.

First Edition: June 2019

Previously published in Korean by Urim Books, Seoul, Korea in 2015

Edited by Dr. Geumsun Vin
Designed by Editorial Bureau of Urim Books
For more information contact at urimbook@hotmail.com

"You see that faith was working with his works,
and as a result of the works, faith was perfected;
and the Scripture was fulfilled which says,
'And Abraham believed God,
and it was reckoned to him as righteousness,'
and he was called

the friend of God."

James 2:22-23

· A Message on Publication ·

Meeting Abraham, the friend of God

In order to understand the Bible and have faith, one should understand the contents in the book of Genesis, for it is the fundamental part of the Bible. It is the introduction to the whole Bible and it speaks of the history of the redemption of the mankind.

I have accumulated a great deal of fasting and prayers since the opening of the church in order to get the understanding of the book of Genesis. Through the inspiration of the Holy Spirit, God revealed to me the secrets of the spiritual realm contained in Genesis, and I delivered them in the sermons.

These sermons have been being broadcast all over the world via TV and Internet, and the contents about Abraham from those sermons have been recently compiled as a book.

Abraham's passing the test of giving Isaac as a burnt offering, being called the friend of God and becoming the Father of Faith is as interesting as watching a TV series. But Abraham did not come to have faith to please God overnight.

> *"You see that faith was working with his works, and as a result of the works, faith was perfected; and the Scripture was fulfilled which says, 'And Abraham believed God, and it was reckoned to him as righteousness,' and he was called the friend of God"* (James 2:22-23).

Abraham obeyed immediately when God commanded him to leave his homeland, his father's house and go to the place where God would show him. As a descendant of Shem, he heard about God from his forefathers, and he obeyed immediately. But when he moved to Egypt from the land of Canaan to escape from famine, he said his wife Sarah was his sister, in order to avoid any problem.

He repented of not relying on God completely only after his wife was taken by the Egyptian king. Through this incident, Abraham came to have the faith to rely on God completely. It was a chance for him to become more intimate with God.

It is not that Abraham had perfect faith from the beginning.

Through trials, he came to have greater faith even to believe in God who could raise a person from the dead. As a result, he was able to pass the test to give his only son Isaac as a burnt offering. He heard the voice of God and understood His heart through deep prayers, so he believed in God who could raise his son from the dead and obeyed His command perfectly.

Jesus said in John 15:13-14, *"Greater love has no one than this, that one lay down his life for his friends. You are My friends if you do what I command you."*

True friends can give anything they have to each other, even their lives. The reason why Abraham could give even his only son, who was more precious than his life itself, was because he deeply loved God. And since God, the master of all things in heaven and earth, accepted his faith and love with joy and acknowledged him as His friend, how tremendously blessed he is! Abraham lived a life with the greatest happiness and blessing that one can enjoy on this earth.

Abraham pleased God with perfect faith and love and he was called a friend of God. Through his acts he became the Father of Faith, and the source of blessing. His footsteps give us many lessons even at this end time.

As the days go by, we are living in a world where love has cooled down and where it is very difficult to find true faith. But those who love God will live according to God's words in any circumstances.

This book will tell us, through Abraham's life, what it is to love God and what it is to act with faith, and what kinds of blessings such acts will bring to us. To the extent that our spiritual faith grows with our love for God, we can become the light and salt of the world and give glory to God. We will then receive God's love and blessings.

I hope the readers will take after the example of Abraham's faith, so that all things will go well with them and they will be healthy, even as their souls prosper, and they will go into the glorious positions in Heaven shining like the sun.

I give thanks to Senior Deaconess Geumsun Vin, the Director of Editorial Bureau and her staff who made the publication of this book possible. I give all thanks and glory to God the Father who has given us delicate love in leading us to publish this book.

October 2015,

Jaerock Lee

· Introduction ·

Main characters in this book

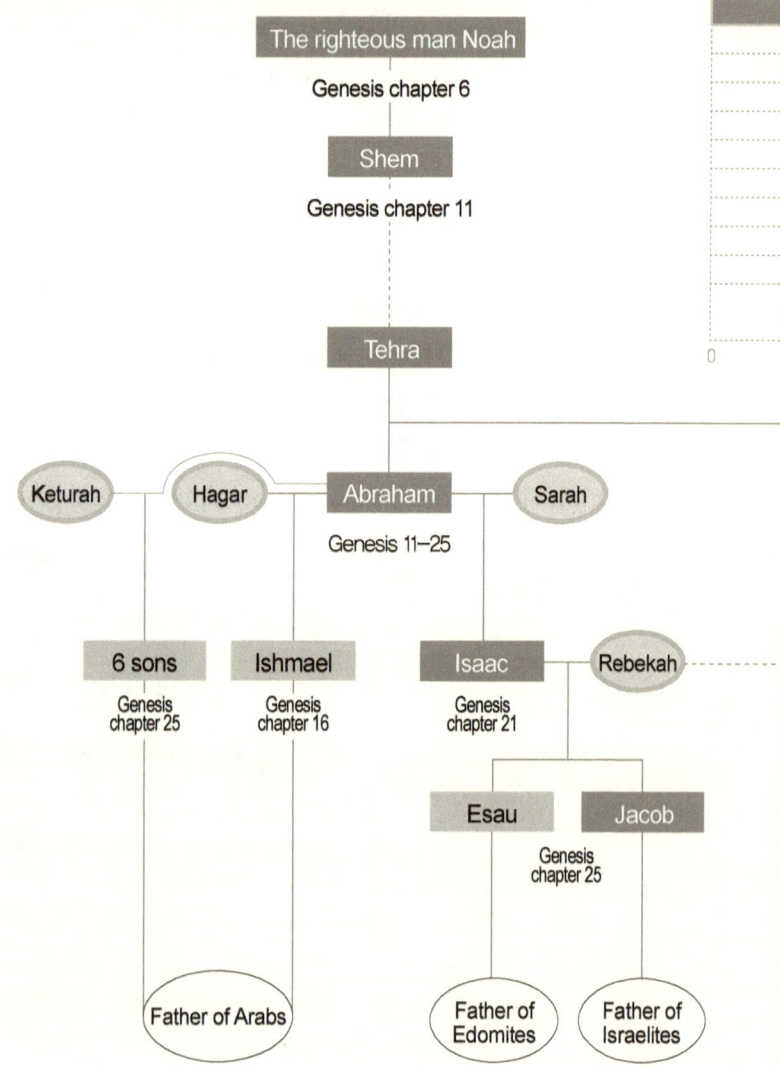

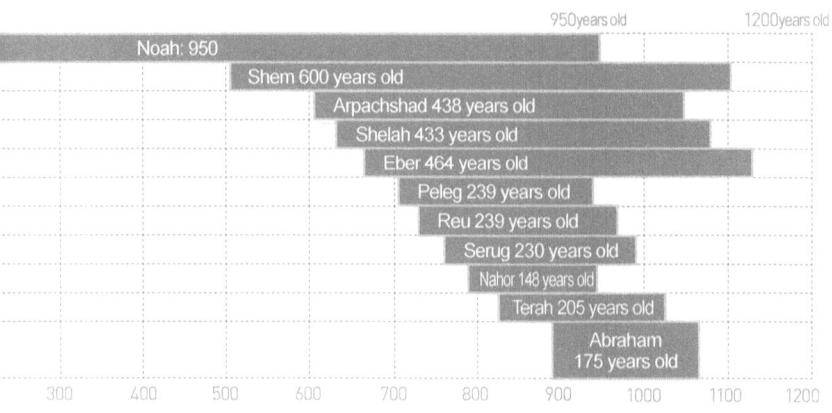

Genealogy of Abraham according to the age of Noah

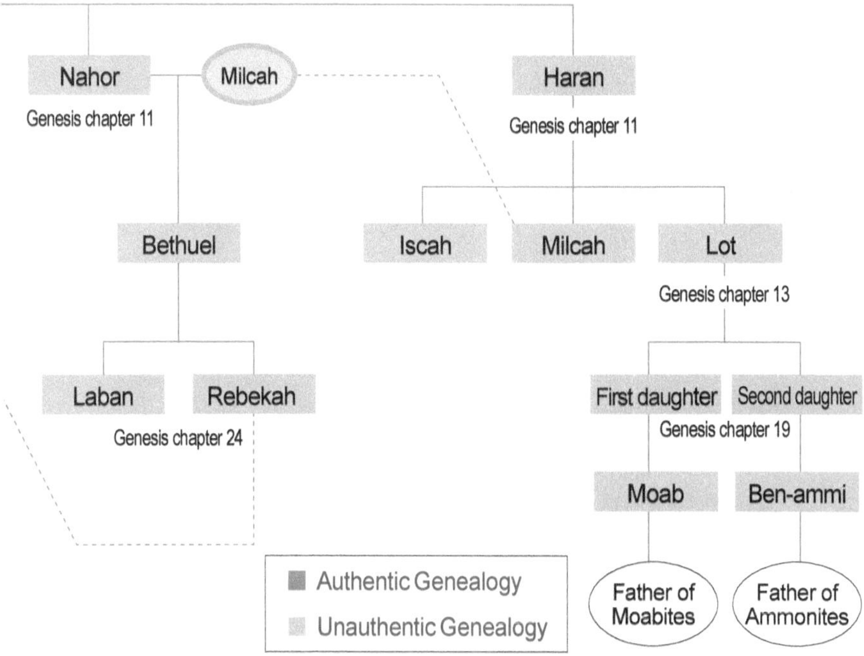

950years old
1200years old
Noah: 950
Shem 600 years old
Arpachshad 438 years old
Shelah 433 years old
Eber 464 years old
Peleg 239 years old
Reu 239 years old
Serug 230 years old
Nahor 148 years old
Terah 205 years old
Abraham 175 years old
300
400
500
600
700
800
900
1000
1100
1200

Nahor
Milcah
Haran
Genesis chapter 11
Genesis chapter 11
Bethuel
Iscah
Milcah
Lot
Genesis chapter 13
Laban
Rebekah
Genesis chapter 24
First daughter
Second daughter
Genesis chapter 19
Moab
Ben-ammi
Authentic Genealogy
Unauthentic Genealogy
Father of Moabites
Father of Ammonites

Contents

A Message on Publication
Introduction

Part 1 Trust and Obedience

Chapter 1 God's Calling and the Trial of Faith · 3

1. God's calling and the covenant of blessing
2. Going to Canaan in obedience
3. "I will give this land to your descendants"
4. Abraham's wife taken from him in Egypt
5. Passing the trial of faith by thorough repentance

Chapter 2 Abraham Relied on God Completely · 19

1. Return to Canaan from Egypt
2. Abram gave the right of first choice to his nephew Lot
3. Lot moved to Sodom to serve his personal interests
4. Moving to Hebron in God's blessing

In Addition 1 - Differences in the Vessels of Heart

Chapter 3 The Rescue of Lot and the Blessing of Melchizedek · 37

    1. The war in the land of Canaan
    2. Rescuing Lot and the people of Sodom and Gomorrah
    3. Giving the tithe to Melchizedek
    4. Declining the offer of spoils of war from the king of Sodom

    # In Addition 2 - Who is Melchizedek, the King of Salem?

Chapter 4 The Righteousness of Faith and God's Promise · 57

    1. The promise of the blessing of descendants
    2. A Burnt offering with blemish-free sacrifice
    3. Showing the future through a dream
    4. From the river of Egypt as far as the great river, the river Euphrates

    # In Addition 3 - Difference between Visions in Old and New Testaments

Chapter 5 Hagar's Conception and the Birth of Ishmael · 79

    1. Sarai gives her maid Hagar as a concubine
    2. Solving the conflict caused by Hagar's conception of Ishmael
    3. Hagar meets a God who sees
    4. Abram begets Ishmael at age 86

Chapter 6 God's Eternal Covenant and the Sign of Circumcision · 93

    1. Walk before Me and be blameless
    2. You will be the father of a multitude of nations
    3. The circumcision for the fulfillment of covenant
    4. The prophecy on Isaac's birth
    5. Every man was circumcised

Part 2 Sacrifice and Submission

Chapter 7 "Shall I hide from Abraham what I am about to do?" · 113

   1. The three persons by the oak of Mamre
   2. Is anything too difficult for the LORD?
   3. Revealing the imminent destruction of Sodom and Gomorrah
   4. The intercession offered with love and in justice

   \# In Addition 4 - What does 'Behold, three men' mean?

Chapter 8 The Two Archangels and Lot's Salvation · 133

   1. The arrival and receiving of the two archangels in Sodom
   2. The corrupt Sodomites and the two archangels
   3. The two archangels bring Lot and his family out
   4. God saves Lot in consideration of Abraham
   5. The judgment of fire on Sodom and Gomorrah
   6. Fathers of Moab and Ammon

   \# In Addition 5 - The Four Living Creatures Executed the Judgment of Fire on Sodom and Gomorrah

Chapter 9   God Reveals Abraham in His Providence · 159

    1. Abimelech takes Abraham's wife Sarah
    2. "Restore the man's wife, for he is a prophet"
    3. Abimelech king of Gerar's apology and compensation
    4. Abimelech receives an answer by Abraham's prayer

Chapter 10   Isaac the Promised Seed and Ishmael · 167

    1. Isaac was born to Abraham at the age of 100
    2. Ishmael mocked Isaac
    3. Hagar and Ishmael sent out into the wilderness
    4. Ishmael takes an Egyptian wife
    5. Abraham and Abimelech made a covenant
    6. Seven ewe lambs as a witness of digging the well

Chapter 11   The Blessings of Jehovah Jireh on Abraham · 187

    1. Giving Isaac as a burnt offering
    2. Taking Isaac to Mount Moriah
    3. Complete obedience of Abraham and Isaac
    4. "Now I know that you fear God"
    5. God prepares a ram for the burnt offering
    6. Established as the Father of Faith
    7. A wife for Isaac, the promised seed

    # In Addition 6 - The Distinction between Subordination, Obedience and Submission

Part 3 Love and Blessings

Chapter 12 Sarah's Death and the Cave of Machpelah · 211

1. Abraham mourns his wife Sarah's death
2. Walking the right way
3. Declining the offer, understanding man's heart
4. Buying the cave of Machpelah for funeral

Chapter 13 Abraham's Old Servant and Isaac's Wife, Rebekah · 225

1. The old servant sets off to look for the wife for Isaac
2. Making an oath with trust in his master Abraham
3. Meeting Rebekah by the guidance of God
4. Telling his story in Rebekah's house
5. Isaac and Rebekah to be married
6. Isaac takes Rebekah as his wife

In Addition 7 - Abraham's Old Servant's Attitude and Heart

Chapter 14 Death of Abraham, Father of Faith and His Duty · 249

1. Descendants of the six sons born of Keturah
2. Isaac succeeds the orthodox genealogy
3. Abraham's death and burial

In Addition 8 - Abraham entered New Jerusalem, the most beautiful heavenly dwelling place

"My Father, my Father,
You have been guiding my whole life.
In all my days, I was guided by You,
and I have been in Your love.

My Father, my Father,
I thank You that You let me live
only according to Your will.

I give thanks to my Father
who has guided me to a life of glory
gained through the eyes of faith
and willingness to obey.

When You wanted something,
You let me know what it was and obey.
I give thanks that You guided me to be blameless.

Part 1

Trust and Obedience

The first step to become the friend of God

Part 1

The magnitude of each individual's trust in God and obedience towards Him is different.

There are some people to whom God has to say something only once and they obey unconditionally. There are others who obey very reluctantly, and still others do not obey at all.

Abraham, the Father of Faith, obeyed immediately and unconditionally when God said anything.

Chapter 1

God's Calling and the Trial of Faith

God's calling and the covenant of blessing
Going to Canaan in obedience
"I will give this land to your descendants"
Abraham's wife taken from him in Egypt
Passing the trial of faith by thorough repentance

1. God's calling and the covenant of blessing

> *"Now the LORD said to Abram, 'Go forth from your country, and from your relatives and from your father's house, to the land which I will show you; and I will make you a great nation, and I will bless you, and make your name great; and so you shall be a blessing; and I will bless those who bless you, and the one who curses you I will curse. And in you all the families of the earth will be blessed'"* (12:1-3).

About 4,000 years ago, Abram (Abraham) was born in Ur of Chaldeans. He was a descendant of Shem, son of Noah (Genesis 11:10-28). Ur was located downstream from the confluence of the Euphrates and Tigris rivers that was the birthplace of Mesopotamian civilization, in the area of Iraq and the southwestern part of Iran today. The land was fertile and people enjoyed affluent lives. It was the center for agriculture, manufacturing industry, and fisheries.

Now what kind of an environment was Abram raised in? At the time Abram was born, his great grandfather Noah and grandfather Shem were all alive.

His great, great grandfathers Shelah and Eber were both alive until Abraham died at the age of 175. In this kind of environment, from a very young age, Abram learned about God and His will and providence through his ancestors. He was raised in a family that revered God. This way, his faith and love for God was also able to grow.

Abram's father Terah gave birth to Abram, Nahor, and Haran. After growing up, Abram married Sarai, and Nahor and Milcah married to start a family respectively. Haran gave birth to Lot and died at an early age. Sarai, Abram's wife was a very beautiful woman but could not bear a child for a long time.

One day Terah wanted to move to the land of Canaan. He left his homeland along with Abram, Sarai, and his nephew Lot whose father had already died. But on his way to Canaan, he settled at a place called Haran. At that time, idolatry was prevalent not only in Ur of Chaldeans but also in Haran.

Terah had been keeping the genuine blood of the family and revered God, but he began to be taken by the tide of the world surrounding him (Joshua 24:2). At this point in time, God let

Abram become independent from his father's house. This was so that Abram would not be stained by the trend of the world there. At the same time, it was the beginning of the trials for Abram that were allowed for him to become the 'Father of Faith'.

Henceforth Abram's walk of faith began. Abram loved God and feared Him, and he had the faith to be able to obey the words of God unconditionally. Now, God commanded Abram to "Go forth from your country, and from your relatives and from your father's house, to the land which I will show you;"

It was not something easy at all to leave his father's house. Going to an unknown destination leaving all the life and family foundations behind is something one can never do if he has any fleshly thoughts.

But Abram easily passed this test. He set out for an unknown and unfamiliar land in obedience without any hesitation. Even though his heart was good and he was raised learning about God, he still had to break down his fleshly thoughts through trials in order for him to reach the level of perfect faith.

The trials allowed for him in the process were not something easy to overcome. After God told Abram to leave his father's house and go to a land which He would show him, God let him know of the blessings that would come upon him if he obeyed.

> *"And I will make you a great nation, and I will bless you, and make your name great; and so you shall be a blessing; and I will bless those who bless you, and the one who curses you I will curse. And in you all the families of the earth will be blessed."*

This promise of blessing wouldn't be realized in an instant. They were going to be given to Abram as he passed all the trials and when he had become established as the 'Father of Faith'. It meant all those words of blessings would be realized on the condition that Abram fulfilled the measure of faith that God wanted him to attain. Abram received this word of blessing with faith and held on to it until he was actually established as the Father of Faith.

2. Going to Canaan in obedience

> *"So Abram went forth as the LORD had spoken to him; and Lot went with him. Now Abram was seventy-five years old when he departed from Haran. Abram took Sarai his wife and Lot his nephew, and all their possessions which they had accumulated,*

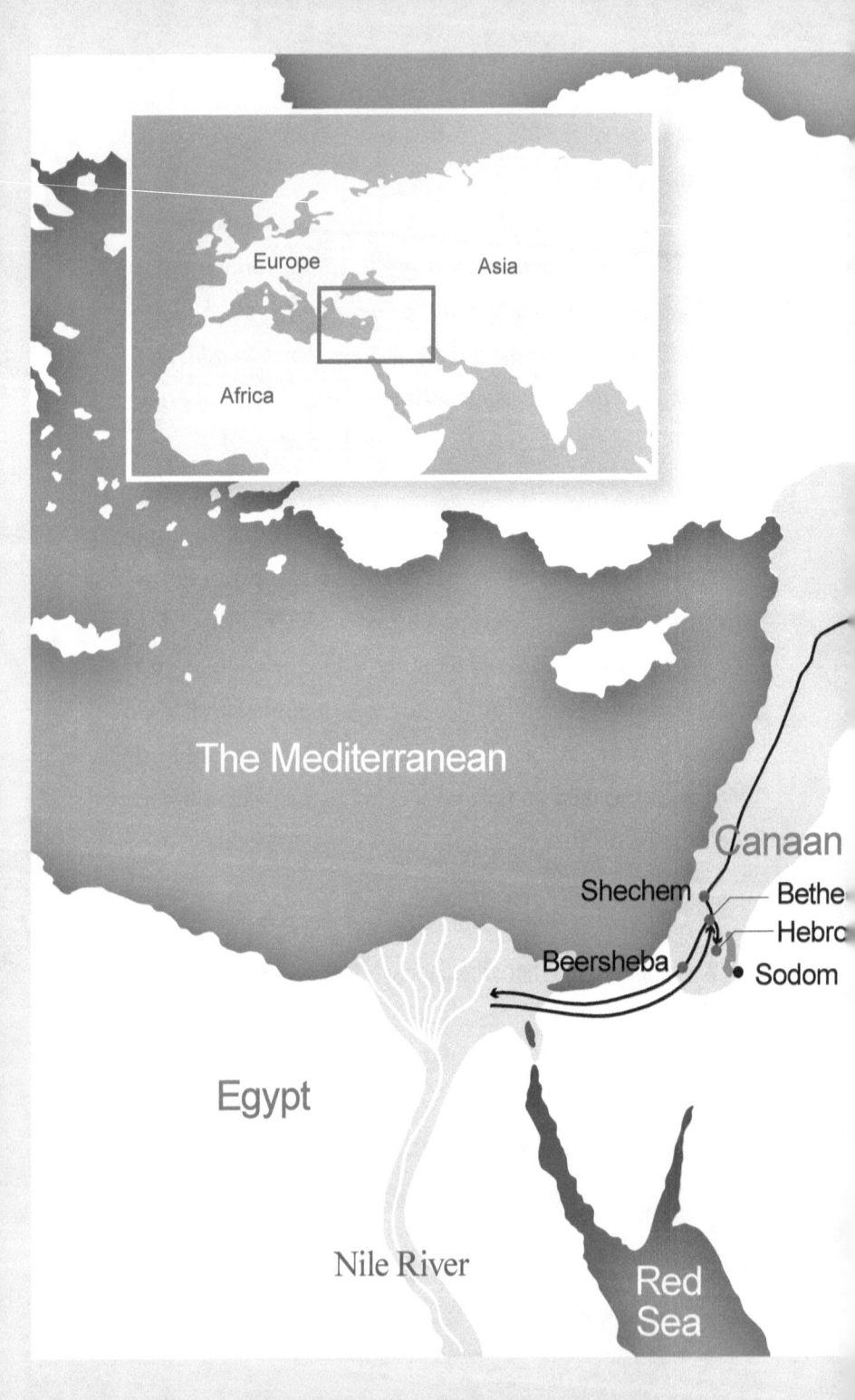

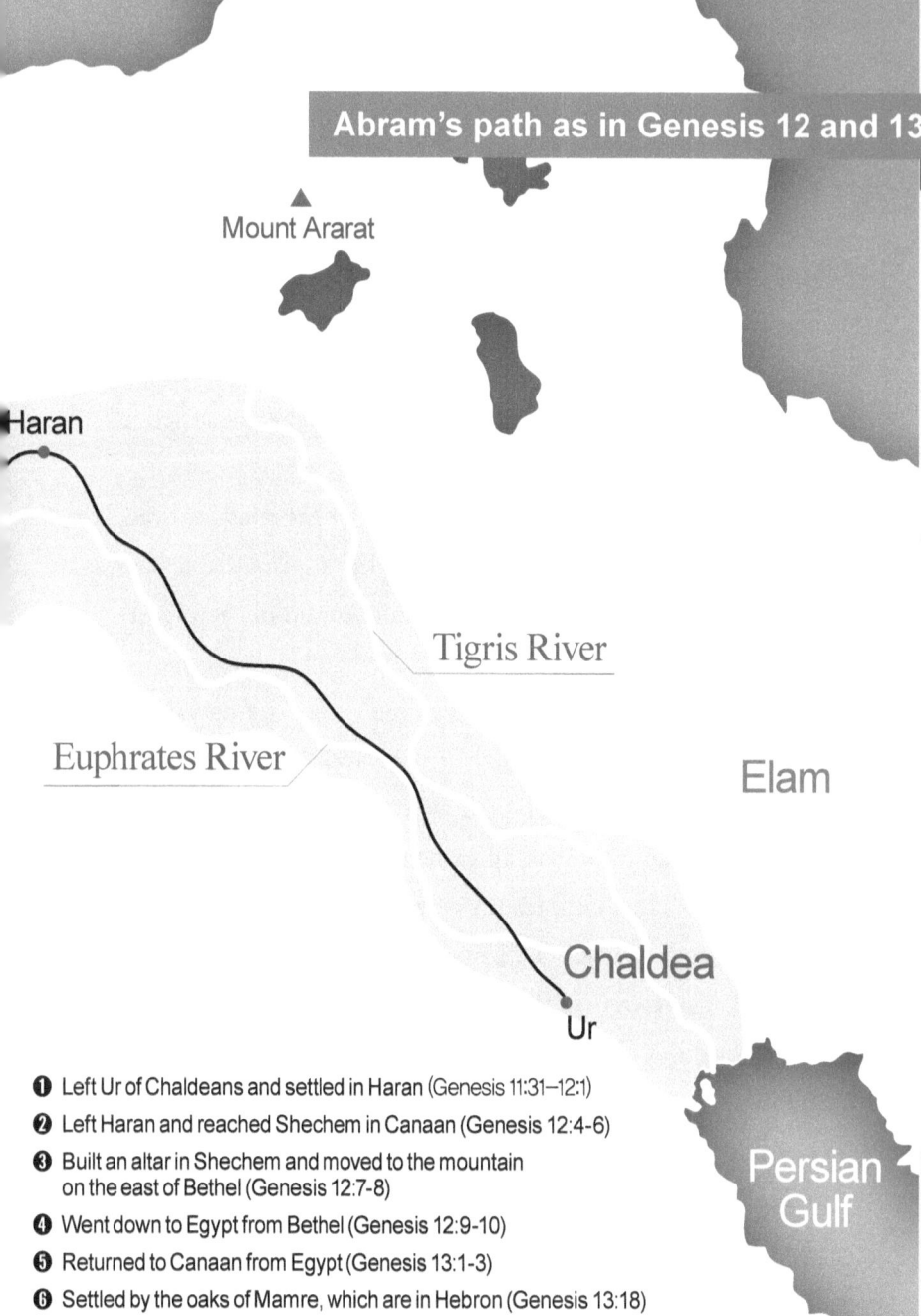

and the persons which they had acquired in Haran, and they set out for the land of Canaan; thus they came to the land of Canaan. Abram passed through the land as far as the site of Shechem, to the oak of Moreh. Now the Canaanite was then in the land" (12:4-6).

Abram was 75 years old when he left Haran, his father's house, in obedience to God's word. His father Terah lived 205 years and Abram lived 175 years. Considering this, 75 years of age might not seem very old. But Abram had already settled in Haran and had all his economic bases there.

Also, Haran was a place where many of his relatives lived, too. It was not something easy at all to leave such a stable base of life to go to an unknown place. But Abram obeyed God's word immediately.

There are people who disobey God's word giving various kinds of excuses, even though it is something that they are more than able to obey. Then, how would they be able to obey the things that are not in agreement with their thoughts or experiences? This is the reason why Abram's obedience stands out, even today. True obedience in God's sight is not just to obey what one can readily obey, but also to obey something that one cannot obey at all, by relying on God and having faith in Him.

Abram brought all his family and possessions that he gained in Haran into the land of Canaan. Eventually he reached the oak at Moreh. Through stable agriculture and commerce, people there were rich. Idol-worship of Baal, Ashtaroth, and Ashera was prevalent. They were sexually and morally corrupt.

3. "I will give this land to your descendants"

"The LORD appeared to Abram and said, 'To your descendants I will give this land.' So he built an altar there to the LORD who had appeared to him. Then he proceeded from there to the mountain on the east of Bethel, and pitched his tent, with Bethel on the west and Ai on the east; and there he built an altar to the LORD and called upon the name of the LORD. Abram journeyed on, continuing toward the Negev" (12:7-9).

Abraham reached the site of Shechem, at the oak of Moreh. God appeared to him and promised that He would give him the land. And, when do you think this promise was fulfilled?

The Old Testament explains in detail that Abram was established as the Father of Faith. Through his descendant, Jacob, a great nation was formed and they went out of Egypt; and eventually they conquered the land of Canaan.

After God has given a certain promise, if those who received it do not obey or lack faith, the fulfillment of the promise might be delayed. It means the word of God will be fulfilled but the point in time of the fulfillment might not be fixed.

For example, when Jesus was healing the sick, most of them were healed then-and-there, and gave glory to God. But in the case of the ten lepers in Luke chapter 17, the lepers were healed on their way to show themselves to the priest, obeying the word of Jesus.

When God promised Abram, *"To your descendants I will give this land,"* it was also fulfilled after a very long time passed. It was fulfilled when the sons of Israel conquered the land of Canaan after the Exodus.

In our Christian lives too, sometimes the answers might not come as quickly as we think they should, or sometimes the circumstances seem to get even worse. Nevertheless, those who believe in the blessings of God and pray unchangingly can certainly experience the works of God. But many people cannot accept the blessing of God with faith. If the answers do not come at the time they want, they begin to doubt and their minds start swaying. Consequently, they do not receive the answer.

4. Abram's wife taken from him in Egypt

"Now there was a famine in the land; so Abram went down to Egypt to sojourn there, for the famine was severe in the land. It came about when he came near to Egypt, that he said to Sarai his wife, 'See now, I know that you are a beautiful woman; and when the Egyptians see you, they will say, "This is his wife"; and they will kill me, but they will let you live. Please say that you are my sister so that it may go well with me because of you, and that I may live on account of you.' It came about when Abram came into Egypt, the Egyptians saw that the woman was very beautiful. Pharaoh's officials saw her and praised her to Pharaoh; and the woman was taken into Pharaoh's house" **(12:10-15)**.

God Himself continued to refine Abram so his faith would reach the full measure. Of course, Abram had loved and revered God from the start. But knowing about God and actually understanding Him through firsthand experience are completely different from each other. For this reason God guided Abram to cultivate perfect faith through refining trials.

Even though one is raised in a very good environment and has learned about God, he still needs to go through trials to have perfect faith that God really wants us to have. It is because he has to cast away unfavorable things related to his personality that he inherited from parents, innate things in his nature, and also all the fleshly things that were input in him without his knowledge in the given circumstances.

Abram passed the first test well, but in order for him to receive the blessings as the Father of Faith, he had to have absolutely no fleshly thoughts. And now he had a chance to demolish his fleshly thoughts completely through a test. It was a test that his wife, Sarai, was taken from him.

Abram was moving southward from Canaan, and because of the famine in the area he went down to Egypt. When he had almost reached Egypt, he thought his life could be in danger because of his wife Sarai. Because Sarai was very beautiful, he thought the Egyptians might kill him to take her away from him.

So, he came up with an idea, which was to say that his wife was his sister. Of course, Sarai was half-sister of Abram, so it was not a complete lie (Genesis 20:12). But the intent in saying so was the problem. It was that Abram did not trust God completely but used his fleshly thoughts that stood against God (Romans 8:6-7).

Abram couldn't even imagine what would happen next. This is the limit of men who cannot see two steps ahead. As a result, Abram saved his life but his wife was taken. She was so beautiful that she was taken by the Pharaoh himself.

Abram knew and believed in the almighty God, but in the

face of an actual test he could not rely on Him completely. Of course, it is not that Abram did anything evil or committed a wrongdoing in the sight of God. If God told him to go down to Egypt without any fear then he would have obeyed with faith. But God did not say anything. He just watched what Abram was doing.

If Abram's faith at that time had reached a little more perfected state, he would have relied on God completely without utilizing his human thoughts, even though God did not tell him anything about what was going to happen. However, Abram's faith had not reached that kind of level yet, and so he came up with his own method in his own wisdom.

For Abram to become the Father of Faith, even the slightest thing about him had to be perfected, so through that incident God revealed his shortcomings, and through this refining trial he realized himself. God of love guided Abram this way so that he would thoroughly realize his shortcomings and go beyond human limits by relying on God alone and completely.

5. Passing the trial of faith by thorough repentance

> "Therefore he treated Abram well for her sake; and gave him sheep and oxen and donkeys and male and female servants and female donkeys and camels. But the LORD struck Pharaoh and

his house with great plagues because of Sarai, Abram's wife. Then Pharaoh called Abram and said, 'What is this you have done to me? Why did you not tell me that she was your wife? Why did you say, "She is my sister," so that I took her for my wife? Now then, here is your wife, take her and go.' Pharaoh commanded his men concerning him; and they escorted him away, with his wife and all that belonged to him" (12:16-20).

Because he had obtained Sarai, Pharaoh, the king of Egypt, treated Abram well. He gave Abram sheep and oxen and donkeys and male and female servants and female donkeys and camels. But since his wife was taken due to his fleshly thoughts, Abram was in agony.

His life was spared, but how could he be at ease? He must have suffered so much thinking about his wife. Now he had nothing he could do but rely on God. He realized his thoughts and his wisdom were wrong and foolish, and thus he repented thoroughly before God.

Anyone who has not yet been fully matured in his faith like Abraham can make mistakes. But the problem is the attitude after making a mistake. Those who acknowledge their faults, turn from their ways, and rely on God will have a very different outcome than those who just keep on acting in their own thoughts.

Abram realized his foolishness and immediately repented. He went before God who could solve all kinds of problems. God heard Abram's prayer and opened a way out (1 Corinthians 10:13).

God struck Pharaoh and his household with a big plague. Not just Pharaoh but also everyone who belonged to him suffered from a disease. Surprised, Pharaoh tried to find out why such a plague came upon him. He realized it was due to Sarai whom he had taken from Abram and called for him in haste.

Eventually the Pharaoh returned Abram's wife to him along with all that belonged to him saying, *"Why did you say, 'She is my sister,' so that I took her for my wife?"* Abram received his wife back at once by completely repenting.

Furthermore, he came out of Egypt with everything that the Pharaoh had given him – sheep and oxen and donkeys and male and female servants and female donkeys and camels. When Abram tried to deal with the problem with his own wisdom, it only became more entangled. But through the intervention of God, not only the problem was solved but also could he gain much more possessions than when he went to Egypt.

Abram passed each of the trials of faith one by one. Later, he would have accumulated enough trust in God even to believe in God who would bring the dead back to life. In this way, he could obey without hesitation even the test to give his only son Isaac as a burnt offering.

Such trust cannot be established overnight. It cannot be established just because you know about someone very well. It can be established after we interact with another person for a long period of time, feeling each other's faithfulness, integrity, and loyalty. It's the same with our relationship with God. The reason why Abram could later obey the command to give his son Isaac as a burnt offering was because he cultivated trust in God while passing the trials of faith one by one.

Chapter 2

Abraham Relied on God Completely

Return to Canaan from Egypt

Abram gave the right of first choice to his nephew Lot

Lot moved to Sodom to serve his personal interests

Moving to Hebron in God's blessing

1. Return to Canaan from Egypt

"So Abram went up from Egypt to the Negev, he and his wife and all that belonged to him, and Lot with him. Now Abram was very rich in livestock, in silver and in gold. He went on his journeys from the Negev as far as Bethel, to the place where his tent had been at the beginning, between Bethel and Ai, to the place of the altar which he had made there formerly; and there Abram called on the name of the LORD" (13:1-4).

Abram returned to Canaan from Egypt with his wife Sarai, all that belonged to him, and his nephew Lot. Through the trial of his wife being taken from him in Egypt, he gained a deep understanding in his heart about God whom he had previously only heard and learned about. The fruit of his experience was enormous.

It led him to realize his 'self' and demolish it completely so he could rely on God completely. Furthermore, in passing this trial he received material blessings, too. His livestock and silver and gold became abundant. This was another intention of God allowing this trial of faith to take place.

The reason why God allows us to go through such trials is not to give us a hard time, but to give us blessings. However, in order to receive spiritual and material blessings like in Abram's case, we have to pass the trials with joy and thanksgiving.

Abram rejoiced and gave thanks even in the midst of the trial of his wife being taken from him. Of course, he was in agony about the fact that his wife was taken away because he had used his own thoughts and wisdom. But he did not resent or complain against God thinking: 'Why would such a trial come upon me? Why didn't God protect me?' But rather, he only received the trial allowed by God with joy and thanksgiving. That is why he received great spiritual blessing.

And as in the rule that states, 'all things will prosper even as our soul prospers', material blessings also followed his trial. Abram came out of Egypt with many more possessions than when he entered. This was also in the plan of God.

When Abram left Haran in obedience to the word of God, he did not have much wealth. So, through this trial, God let Abram's soul prosper and gave him material blessing as well. To make this happen, God used the Pharaoh, the most powerful man in Egypt. The blessing after the trial would be great because it would come through the most powerful man of all Egypt.

In this way, God gives us blessings both in spirit and body with wisdom and methods that men cannot fathom. If a trial is allowed due to some wrongdoings or evil acts, there won't be any blessings even if the individual repents and turns from his ways. He will just recover his previous state.

However, if the trial is allowed for spiritual blessing and not due to some evil acts or wrongdoings, then the latter state will be much greater than the former if one passes the trial. This was the case with Abram. When he realized his weakness and relied on God completely, God made him richer than before.

After returning to Canaan from Egypt, Abram once again built an altar where he had built an altar when he had first entered Canaan (Genesis 12:8). He realized the delicate and gentle heart of God that he had not realized before. So, he offered a sacrifice of thanksgiving to God who had saved him in the test and gave him greater wealth than before.

He did not just say vainly, "God, thank You, I realized this and that." By building the altar he showed that his profession and realization were true. He once again engraved in his heart his profession of thanksgiving and offered his thankful heart as a beautiful aroma before God.

God does not simply accept all the thanksgiving of men just because they casually give thanks. God will accept the aroma of the heart and acknowledge their thanksgiving only when they offer it with the acceptable aroma of thanks before God. When God acknowledges our thanksgiving this way, it will be stored up in Heaven.

When God said to Abram that He would give the land to him and his descendants as recorded in Genesis 12:7, Abram built an altar there to God. By giving sacrifices on the altar, he confirmed with God once again the covenant that God had given to him.

In trials, we might feel we have nobody to turn to and there is no way out. But after passing the trial well, we will see that our faith has grown very much. This was the case with Abram, as well.

When he was once again building an altar in the place where he had built an altar before, his heart was very different than his heart in the past. Of course, even in the past, he diligently built altars before God, but he was just practicing what he had learned from his ancestors. He just followed what he had been taught, which is that he had to build altars in certain occasions. But now, he built an altar with all his heart and praised the holy name of God with thanksgiving.

After Abram underwent the trial a dramatic change took place in him. Through just this one trial he was changed very much. His love and trust in God came close to the level that God could acknowledge. Now, he came to commit everything into God's will and guidance.

2. Abram gave the right of first choice to his nephew Lot

> *"Now Lot, who went with Abram, also had flocks and herds and tents. And the land could not sustain them while dwelling together, for their possessions were so great that they were not able to remain together. And there was strife between the herdsmen of Abram's livestock and the herdsmen of Lot's livestock. Now the Canaanite and the Perizzite were dwelling then in the land. So Abram said to Lot, 'Please let there be no strife between you and me, nor between my herdsmen and your herdsmen, for we are brothers. Is not the whole land before you? Please separate from me; if to the left, then I will go to the right; or if to the right, then I will go to the left'"* **(Genesis 13:5-9).**

By the time Abram and Lot left Egypt, they were both already very rich. They had large numbers of livestock and many people in the household. However, there was a problem. They had so many possessions that they could not stay together any longer. Due to the shortage of water and land to feed their herds, the herdsmen of Abram and those of Lot sometimes had quarrels.

So, Abram made a suggestion to Lot saying, *"Please let there be no strife between you and me, nor between my herdsmen and your herdsmen, for we are brothers. Is not the whole land before you? Please separate from me; if to the left, then I will go to the right; or if to the right, then I will go to the left."* He gave up the right to choose first. He yielded it to his nephew Lot.

This tells us that Abram's faith had matured after the trials. He did not seek his own interests and advantage, but yielded to his nephew the right to choose the better land. This kind of faith was made through the trials and hardships. This also shows us that Abram relied on God alone.

When Abram left Haran, Lot had no choice but to just follow his uncle because he did not have any wealth and he was not able to be independent. But now, he accumulated a lot of wealth and he could not stay with Abram any longer. This means Lot received a lot of blessings because he stayed with Abram. God protected Lot's possessions along with Abram's because he belonged with Abram. That is why his wealth increased.

Considering this, what should Lot have done when there was strife between his herdsmen and Abram's herdsmen? Of course he should have backed off because he was a nephew. It was the right course of action.

But Lot would not do so. When he was given the right of first choice, he chose the good land without hesitation. This was not appropriate at all. In a spiritual sense it was even more inappropriate.

Lot should have served Abram even more in the spiritual sense. Yet, he did not. We can see that he neither understood nor did he give thanks for the blessings he had received through Abram.

Even in this situation, Abram did not say anything to Lot like, "You became wealthy and have been protected by God because of me." Abram did not have any resentment or hard feelings.

3. Lot moved to Sodom to serve his personal interests

> "Lot lifted up his eyes and saw all the valley of the Jordan, that it was well watered everywhere—this was before the LORD destroyed Sodom and Gomorrah—like the garden of the LORD, like the land of Egypt as you go to Zoar. So Lot chose for himself all the valley of the Jordan, and Lot journeyed eastward. Thus they separated from each other. Abram settled in the land of Canaan, while Lot settled in the cities of the valley, and moved his tents as far as Sodom. Now the men of Sodom were wicked exceedingly

and sinners against the LORD" (13:10-13).

The Jordan Valley that Lot chose was like the garden of the LORD. It was like the land of Egypt. An interesting fact here is that this good land was likened to the land in Egypt. What is the reason for this? We might have a question about it if we think of the land of Egypt as it is today. However, through this record, we can see how fertile and affluent the land of Egypt was at the time of Abram.

The first man Adam, when he was living in the Garden of Eden, often came down to this earth. One of his favorite spots was the land of Egypt. The exotic nature and beautiful environment there was charming enough even to suit Adam who was living in the Garden of Eden at the time. And because the land that Lot chose had enough water and was fertile, it too was likened to the land of Egypt.

Lot chose the land that looked abundant and finally he reached Sodom. Lot left Abram to seek his own interests and ignored the spiritual order. He kept on falling into pit after pit without knowing the reason why they were coming upon him.

The land was so stained by sins that the Bible says, *"Now the men of Sodom were wicked exceedingly and sinners against the LORD."* Lot willingly went into the land because he was not being guided by God. Spiritual and physical idolatry, adultery and sexual immorality permeated all Sodom. Because of that influence, grave sins in the sight of God were prevalent in the sensual and morally corrupt culture.

After the incident of the Tower of Babel in Genesis 11, languages were divided and people dispersed. They formed different groups and races. On the one hand, some of them continued their lineage revering God and keeping their orthodoxy in the choosing of God. On the other hand, some others forgot the existence of God and indulged themselves in idolatry and pleasure following their lust. One of the best examples of such a place was Sodom. It came about that Lot reached Sodom because he was following the flesh.

People make many choices in exercising their freewill. They have to choose what to eat, what to wear, whether to attend Sunday service or just take a rest, whether to seek personal benefit and interests or to make sacrifices and yield themselves for others.

Whatever we choose, it is up to us. But depending on our choices, we might be led to happiness or we may shed tears of sorrow and regret. If we follow our own desires like Lot, we will face trials and pain, but if we obey the Word of God like Abram, we will be guided to the way of blessings.

4. Moving to Hebron in God's blessing

"The LORD said to Abram, after Lot had separated from him, 'Now lift up your eyes and look from the place where you are, northward and southward and eastward and westward; for all the land which you see, I will give it to you and to your descendants forever. I will make your descendants as the dust of the earth, so that if anyone can number the dust of the earth, then your descendants can also be numbered. Arise, walk about the land through its length and breadth; for I will give it to you.' Then Abram moved his tent and came and dwelt by the oaks of Mamre, which are in Hebron, and there he built an altar to the LORD" (13:14-18)

Lot left Abram and got himself into more difficulties, but on the other hand, Abram received increasingly more blessings. This could also mean that Abram may have been able to receive even greater blessings had Lot not previously been with him.

For example, suppose there is a family member who is lovely in the sight of God and who deserves to receive blessings from God. But because all the other members don't deserve to receive blessings, as a whole family they can't receive the blessings fully. Of course, God will bless the beloved persons individually, but He can't bless the whole family. In this case, if this beloved person becomes independent, God can bless him fully and individually, and to the full extent that he deserves to receive blessings.

This principle can be applied in all the other aspects. If you work with a person who is not right in the sight of God, the blessing that is supposed to come to you might be blocked. It hinders your soul from becoming prosperous. It becomes an obstacle to you to receive blessings. But it does not mean you should indiscriminately shun unbelievers. It just means you should not take up sides or unite with those who follow evil.

Lot knew God, but he was not right in the sight of God in some aspects. That is why God blessed Abram even more after Lot had left Abram. But it does not mean Lot was worse than any ordinary person. He also learned the truth being with Abram and he tried to live a righteous life, too (2 Peter 2:8). Nevertheless, he lacked so much compared to Abram and departed from Abram following his own interests.

After Lot left, God said to Abram, *"Now lift up your eyes and look from the place where you are, northward and southward and eastward and westward; for all the land which you see, I will give it to you and to your descendants forever."*

This promise also includes what God would do through the sons of Israel who are the descendants of Abram. The nation of Israel, the chosen people of God, would be formed through the genealogy of Abram. God would set Israel high above all nations to make the name of the LORD God known widely.

This promise carries the meaning that God would make Himself known all over the world through Israel and fulfill the providence of human cultivation. And, Abram was the person God had chosen to fulfill this grand plan and providence. For this reason God promised Abram such great love and blessings. But this promise of blessing was not only for Abram individually, but also for the whole nation of Israel. That is why the promise was something very big.

God said, *"...for all the land which you see, I will give it to you and to your descendants forever."* This is not just a promise that God would give them the land that he could see. It is a promise that even includes the providence of salvation for them. In order to fulfill this promise, God let the Savior come forth through Israel, and when the time was right at the end time, He let the gospel return to Israel through the works of the Holy Spirit.

Now, God gives Abram more specific information. He said, *"I will make your descendants as the dust of the earth, so that if anyone can number the dust of the earth, then your descendants can also be numbered."* It is an elaboration as to how God would fulfill the promise in Genesis 12:2, which was the word of God when He called Abram for the first time. It is written, *"And I will make you a great nation, and I will bless you, and make your name great; and so you shall be a blessing."* It means just as it is impossible to number the dust of the earth, Abram's descendants would multiply so much that it wouldn't be possible to number them.

It reveals how many descendants would come forth in the future through Abram. The descendants here do not refer to biological genealogy but the descendants of faith.

Abram would become the 'father of nations' and the Father of Faith. He would be the father of all believers. Therefore, up until this day, all those who have been saved by faith are his descendants. Abram will have the honor of being the father in faith every time there is a person who is saved by faith.

This blessing of God given to Abram was by no means a small blessing. It is the blessing that has existed but once throughout the entire history of mankind. Of course, this promise was going to be fulfilled when Abram passed all the tests to become perfect in the sight of God. God gave him this word of promise because He knew Abram would do it. Abram also held on to this word of promise firmly with faith, and this word of God was fulfilled as spoken.

In Addition 1

Differences in the Vessels of Heart

The differences in the vessels of heart in view of gentleness and reasonableness

Anyone can have gentleness and reasonableness to the extent that they cast away sins and evil and change themselves according to the truth that is the Word of God.

Gentleness of heart is a condition of the heart that allows us to give up everything we have because the truth abounds in our heart and at the same time we have the freedom of the truth. Reasonableness of heart is the condition of the heart that is good and beautiful. It is to be OK with either choice within the truth, but seeks to choose the side that pleases God more. Those who have reasonableness bear the good fruit of their lips and beautiful fruit of their deeds.

Abram had both gentleness and reasonableness. We can see this from the fact that he yielded the right of first choice to his nephew, Lot. As a matter of fact, Lot had received the blessings he received only thanks to Abram. From the viewpoint of a nephew, what should he have done when he heard there were quarrels among his herdsmen and those of his uncle?

He should have strictly reprimanded his herdsmen so such news wouldn't be heard by his uncle. But Lot's heart was not broad enough to think about his uncle's standpoint. He was only interested in his own possessions. He considered his standpoint first. That is why, when given the right to choose first by his uncle, Lot immediately chose the land that was good in his sight (Genesis 13:10-11).

What if Lot declined his uncle's offer? Even if he had, Abram would have insisted that Lot choose the better land first. But again, even if Abram had insisted once again, Lot should have taken the land that was not better so that Abram could take the better land.

If he declined to choose first several times but eventually chose the good land in his sight just because Abram asked him to do so, then, we cannot say he really followed the right way of men. Of course, it is better than a man who would choose what he'd like right from the beginning. However, if he really understood the grace he received from Abram, he couldn't have chosen the better land even though he had been given the right to choose first.

And now look what Lot had done. He chose the better land without declining Abram's offer even once. We can see the vessel of his heart here very clearly. What do you think Abram's heart was like at that moment? Even though Lot chose the better land first, Abram did not harbor any hard-feelings or resentment. He was just filled with peace and he could just keep on giving. Because he had served even the little ones from his heart, he could yield what he could've enjoyed. He had the generosity to be able to give even more.

The difference of vessels in view of taking the credit for one's work

We can see the difference in the size of the vessel of heart by considering whether one wants to take the credit or let it be given to somebody else for a job well done.

Lot received blessings only because he was with his uncle Abram. But he couldn't even realize it, and thus he couldn't appreciate it either. However, Abram did not try to take the credit for Lot's blessings nor did he resent Lot. Abram had never said, "You received blessings because you are staying with me."

This kind of person is one who has a big vessel of heart. Abram gave all the credit to God, without trying to reveal his work. In fact, how could he receive blessings if God did not protect him and was not with him? Therefore, Abram gave all the glory only to God.

Also, when there were quarrels among the herdsmen, he did not try to put the blame on anybody else. He just took all the responsibility; he had a big vessel of heart. That is why he offered Lot a way for both of them to have peace. It means Abram had the beautiful heart to understand and care for the other person and to pursue peace.

In this situation, Lot just left Abram serving only his own interests and without realizing his fault. If Lot was really a man of God, he'd have had to ask God first for guidance. But he couldn't be guided by God because he was blinded by his greed. As a result, he ended up being caught up in a miserable situation.

Abraham

Chapter 3

The Rescue of Lot and the Blessing of Melchizedek

The war in the land of Canaan
Rescuing Lot and the people of Sodom and Gomorrah
Giving the tithe to Melchizedek
Declining the offer of spoils of war from the king of Sodom

1. The war in the land of Canaan

"And it came about in the days of Amraphel king of Shinar, Arioch king of Ellasar, Chedorlaomer king of Elam, and Tidal king of Goiim, that they made war with Bera king of Sodom, and with Birsha king of Gomorrah, Shinab king of Admah, and Shemeber king of Zeboiim, and the king of Bela (that is, Zoar). All these came as allies to the valley of Siddim (that is, the Salt Sea). Twelve years they had served Chedorlaomer, but the thirteenth year they rebelled. In the fourteenth year Chedorlaomer and the kings that were with him, came and defeated the Rephaim in Ashteroth-karnaim and the Zuzim in Ham and the Emim in Shaveh-kiriathaim, and the Horites in their Mount Seir, as far as El-paran, which is by the wilderness. Then they turned back and came to En-mishpat (that is, Kadesh), and conquered all the country of the Amalekites, and also the Amorites, who lived in Hazazon-tamar. And the king of Sodom and the king of Gomorrah and the king

of Admah and the king of Zeboiim and the king of Bela (that is, Zoar) came out; and they arrayed for battle against them in the valley of Siddim, against Chedorlaomer king of Elam and Tidal king of Goiim and Amraphel king of Shinar and Arioch king of Ellasar four kings against five. Now the valley of Siddim was full of tar pits; and the kings of Sodom and Gomorrah fled, and they fell into them. But those who survived fled to the hill country. Then they took all the goods of Sodom and Gomorrah and all their food supply, and departed. They also took Lot, Abram's nephew, and his possessions and departed, for he was living in Sodom" (14:1-12).

"*...in the days of Amraphel king of Shinar*" refers to the time after the Tower of Babel. It was when people were dispersed according to their languages and races. It was the time socio-political powers began to form. At that time, there were many kings governing their own lands in relatively small areas. They sometimes allied with each other or fought against each other to expand their territories.

In the past, the five kings that were in possession of the Canaan Land, including Sodom and Gomorrah, had lost in the battle against the four kings of the North. They were serving the kings of the North, especially King Chedorlaomer for twelve years. However, in the thirteenth year they rebelled.

Chedorlaomer became enraged. He formed an allied force and went south to Canaan. He defeated Rephaim, Zuzim,

Emim, and Horites. He turned the direction of his assault and defeated the Amalekites and Amorites. Finally, Chedorlaomer entered into a fierce battle against the allied forces of the South at Siddim.

In this battle, the northern allies headed by Chedorlaomer utterly defeated and won great victories against the southern allies of five kings including the King of Sodom. They took not only goods and food supplies, but they took the people as captives as well. In this incident Abram's nephew Lot was also taken and his possessions were taken, too.

2. Rescuing Lot and the people of Sodom and Gomorrah

"Then a fugitive came and told Abram the Hebrew. Now he was living by the oaks of Mamre the Amorite, brother of Eshcol and brother of Aner, and these were allies with Abram. When Abram heard that his relative had been taken captive, he led out his trained men, born in his house, three hundred and eighteen, and went in pursuit as far as Dan. He divided his forces against them by night, he and his servants, and defeated them, and pursued them as far as Hobah, which is north of Damascus. He brought back all the goods, and also brought back his relative Lot with his possessions, and also the women, and the people" **(14:13-16)**

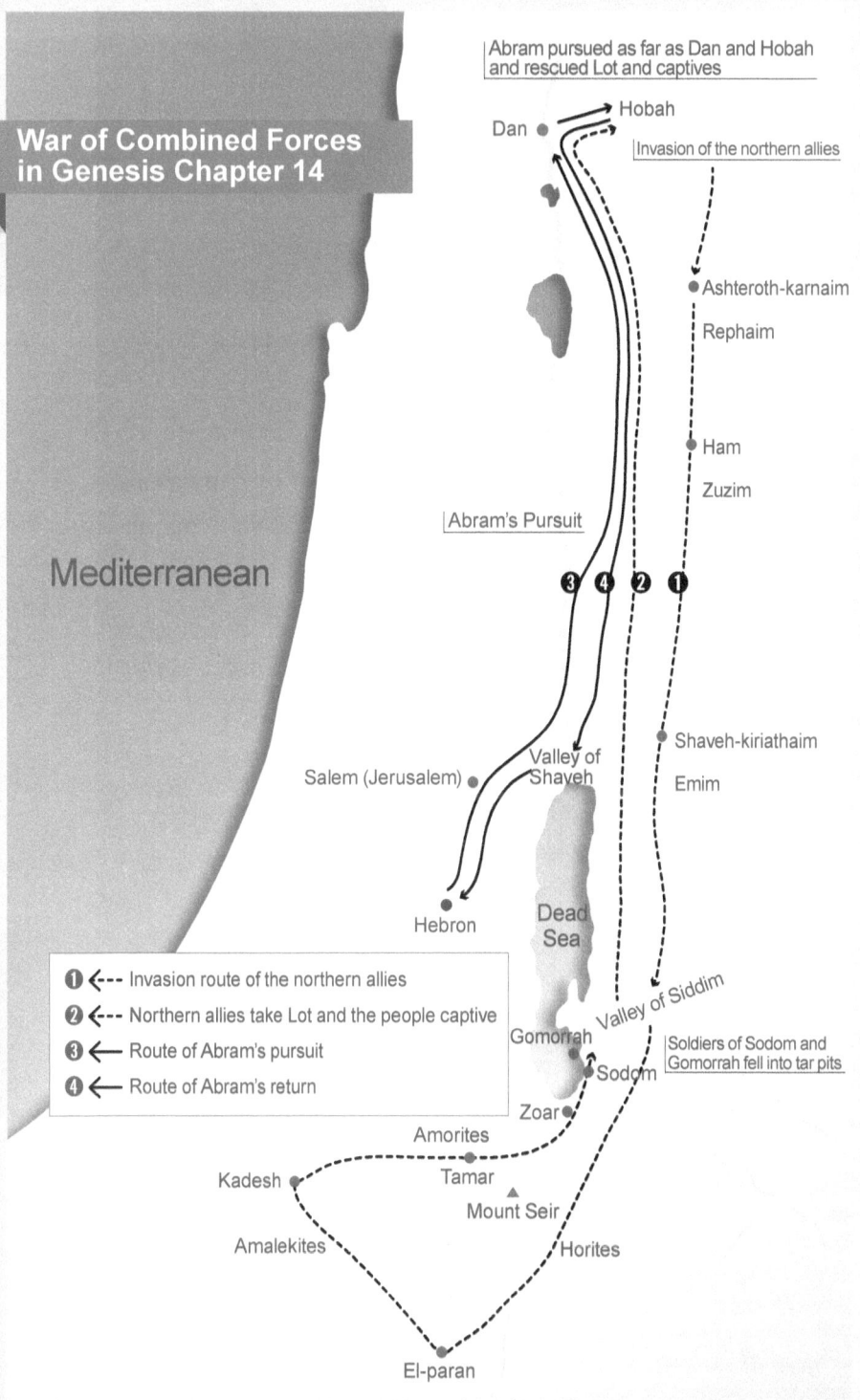

As most parts of the land of Canaan were conquered by the northern allies, what happened to Abram? Verse 13 says, *"Then a fugitive came and told Abram the Hebrew. Now he was living by the oaks of Mamre the Amorite, brother of Eshcol and brother of Aner, and these were allies with Abram."* Even in the turmoil of the war, Abram was not harmed at all. He was safely protected by God.

Abram was living by the oaks of Mamre the Amorite. Even though the Amorites were harmed by the northern allies, Abram who was living near the Amorites was completely protected. Especially in point is that Abram formed allies with influential people around him not just in his own area but in the surrounding areas too. He increased his power by being on good terms with the powers around him.

How was it possible that Abram could be on good terms with all the powers around him? It was because he was protected and guaranteed by God and he always served others. Amorites and other Gentile races wouldn't have had good relationships with Abram right from the beginning. They couldn't do anything to Abram because they had witnessed that God was with him.

Once, Abram's wife was taken by the Pharaoh. The news about what happened next spread widely throughout the land. They all heard about the God who protected Abram and was with him. Also, they could feel the hands of God who was attesting to and blessing Abram. For these reasons they could not maltreat or mistreat Abram.

Furthermore, Abram did not disregard or look down upon the people around him saying something like, "I am a person who is protected by God!" But he rather served them with a good heart. Naturally people around him had good feelings toward him and they came to have healthy relationship.

While Abram was living in peace, dwelling in the land of Canaan, one day a man came to him with urgent news. He informed Abram that his nephew Lot was taken captive in a war. Abram took immediate action. He led out three hundred eighteen of his trained men who were born in his house, and brought back Lot, the possessions that had been taken, and even the people of Sodom and Gomorrah.

It was action taken at the risk of his own life. Even though he was very rich, fighting a war is something quite different. The combined forces of the north had already defeated many kings, and their morale was high.

What is the real reason that Abram could go out and fight? Abram did not look at the reality of the situation. He saw only with the eyes of faith. He had complete trust in God who protected and led him, so he did not care about the number of soldiers he had. He just relied on God and fought bravely. The number of soldiers is important to men but it holds little meaning for God (Psalm 20:7).

In Judges chapter 7, Gideon defeated the combined forces of Midianites, Amalekites, and sons of the east, of which the number was counted 'as many as locusts of the field'. With the wisdom given by God and with His help, the sons of Gideon defeated a great number of the enemy forces with a very small number of soldiers. God let Gideon divide his soldiers into three groups and cause confusion among the enemy soldiers in the middle of the night. The enemy forces killed each other fighting among themselves.

Abram also used a similar tactic to that of Gideon to win the victory. He went out bravely with faith and defeated the enemy force with the wisdom of God. Just as David sought God in every decision he was going to make and received the answers, Abram did not rely on his own wisdom and power but asked God for His guidance.

From this event where Abram rescued Lot from captivity, we can see that Abram is a good person who fulfills his duty to the fullest. If he had just a little bit of evil in him, he could have just ignored the situation thinking, 'Lot has taken the good land as he wished so now he is facing this calamity.' Abram could've thought he had done everything he could and thus was not responsible for anything that happened to Lot. Or maybe, Abram might have gone to rescue his nephew with reluctance.

But Abram took the men trained in his household and went out to rescue Lot without any hesitation. He did not just send his men, either. He did not worry thinking: 'What will happen to my household if I leave my place in this war?' He didn't have time to think about his own possessions when he went out with his men.

Even though Lot left Abram seeking his own benefit, Abram had the good heart to take the responsibility for a person who had once belonged with him.

If you think about the fact that there were 318 men and their families and other necessary people, then you can imagine the great power Abram had at that time. Abram was able to stand out while living among the Gentiles because he laid a firm foundation in his household through the great blessings of God.

What we should understand here is that Abram also had done everything he was supposed to have done. He relied on God completely but it doesn't mean he neglected his duties that he had to do. He did not consider lightly the things he had to do thinking God would protect him. He continuously trained his men in order to keep himself and his possessions safe. For this reason he could set out to rescue Lot immediately.

3. Giving the tithe to Melchizedek

> *"Then after his* [Abram's] *return from the defeat of Chedorlaomer and the kings who were with him, the king of Sodom went out to meet him at the valley of Shaveh (that is, the King's Valley). And Melchizedek king of Salem brought out bread and wine; now he was a priest of God Most High. He blessed him and said, 'Blessed be Abram of God Most High, Possessor of heaven and earth; and blessed be God Most High, who has delivered your enemies into your hand.' He* [Abram] *gave him a tenth of all"* (14:17-20).

Abram defeated the combined forces of Chedorlaomer and the kings with him, and brought back the people and possessions of Sodom and Gomorrah. The king of Sodom came out to meet Abram at the valley of Shaveh and gave thanks, for he had received unexpected help.

Abram built an altar and was offering up prayers of thanksgiving, and Melchizedek, a priest of God Most High, appeared with bread and wine. Melchizedek blessed Abram saying, *"Blessed be Abram of God Most High, Possessor of heaven and earth; and blessed be God Most High, who has delivered your enemies into your hand."*

So, Abram gave a tenth of everything he had gained in the battle. This appearance of Melchizedek, the king of Salem, and the way Abram treated him is not something ordinary. In fact there is a very deep spiritual meaning in it.

The Bible refers to Melchizedek as 'a priest of God Most High'. As a matter of fact, the position of a priest came into existence in Israel from the time of Moses, beginning with his brother Aaron, which was long after Abram's time. God let the sons of Levi, the third son of Jacob fulfill the duty of priests, beginning with Aaron.

But way before the priesthood came into being, Melchizedek, a priest of God Most High appears. Paul wrote about this in Hebrews 7:10, saying, *"...for he was still in the loins of his father when Melchizedek met him."* When Melchizedek met Abram, Levi had not even been born. In other words, there was a special reason why the position of a priest was given to Melchizedek.

Hebrews 7:11 says, *"Now if perfection was through the Levitical priesthood (for on the basis of it the people received the Law), what further need was there for another priest to arise according to the order of Melchizedek, and not be designated according to the order of Aaron?"*

Here, 'order' refers to the grade, rank, or the order of hierarchy. Also, 'another priest according to the order of Melchizedek' refers to Jesus who demolished the wall of sin between God and men by offering Himself as the propitiation for sin. Hebrews 7:15-17 says, *"And this is clearer still, if another priest arises according to the likeness of Melchizedek, who has become such not on the basis of a law of physical requirement, but according to the power of an indestructible life. For it is attested of Him 'You are a priest forever according to the order of Melchizedek.'"*

Jesus did not follow the order of the Levi but was born as a descendant of Judah, yet He still became our Priest. Paul says the basis on which Jesus could do so was in Melchizedek. Psalm 110:4 also says, *"The LORD has sworn and will not change His mind, 'You are a priest forever according to the order of Melchizedek.'"*

Then, who is this Melchizedek who could compare with Jesus, the only begotten Son of God and one with the original God? Please refer to this chapter's post script, 'In Addition 2'.

4. Declining the offer of spoils of war from the king of Sodom

> *"The king of Sodom said to Abram, 'Give the people to me and take the goods for yourself.' Abram said to the king of Sodom, 'I have sworn to the LORD God Most High, possessor of heaven and earth, that I will not take a thread or a sandal thong or anything that is yours, for fear you would say, 'I have made Abram rich.' I will take nothing except what the young men have eaten, and the share of the men who went with me, Aner, Eshcol, and Mamre; let them take their share'"* (14:21-24).

Abram gave the victory to the king of Sodom. The king wanted to give thanks to Abram and offered him the goods that were gained in the war. But Abram refused saying, *"I will not take a thread or a sandal thong or anything that is yours,"* and, *"I will take nothing except what the young men have eaten, and the share of the men who went with me, Aner, Eshcol, and Mamre; let them take their share."*

Abram in fact did a great favor to the king of Sodom by winning the war. Also, the king himself came out to meet Abram and offered him the goods. And yet Abram did not want to take advantage of such a situation. It's because he did not have any desire to seek his own interest or material gain.

He only wanted to receive blessings from God. It means he

became rich not by seeking his own benefits but by the blessing of God, which is given to those whose souls prosper.

There was another reason why Abram declined the king's offer. It's because he knew the hearts of people very well. People can change their minds any time unless their hearts are changed according to the truth. In other words, right now, the king of Sodom is happy and he wants to give Abram something in return, but later, he can say something very different.

For example, he could have said, "I gave some goods to Abram only because he wanted something from me." Knowing such a heart of people, how would Abram be able to accept the offer of the king of Sodom? Abram did not take anything except the food that the men ate and the share that was to be given to other soldiers who went with him. It is also Abram's consideration for the people who worked with him, taking the responsibility and rewarding their hard work.

In Addition 2

Who is Melchizedek, the King of Salem?

Hebrews 6:20 says, *"... where Jesus has entered as a forerunner for us, having become a high priest forever according to the order of Melchizedek."*

If Melchizedek were a creature, it couldn't have been said Jesus, the Son of God, is a high priest 'according to the order of Melchizedek'. In order to be able to say Jesus is a high priest 'according to the order of Melchizedek', Melchizedek has to be at least as high as Jesus.

If Melchizedek is as high as the Son of God, Jesus, then it is clear that He is none other than the Holy Spirit. Some might wonder how it can be that the King of Salem, Melchizedek, is the Holy Spirit.

Here, Salem in Hebrew means 'safe' or 'peaceful'. Later Salem becomes Jerusalem, but in a spiritual sense it refers to the kingdom of God (Psalm 76:1-2; 135:21). Therefore, the King of Salem is the same with God and the ruler in the kingdom of God, namely the Holy Spirit.

Reason Why Melchizedek, King of Salem, is the Holy Spirit

Hebrews 5:10 says that Jesus is a priest according to the order of Melchizedek. But in verse 11 it says, *"Concerning him we have much to say, and it is hard to explain, since you have become dull of hearing."* The apostle Paul, the writer of the book of Hebrews, had an understanding about Melchizedek, but he did not delve into details because it was difficult for other people to understand.

However, Paul still left some clues in Hebrews chapter 7 so that the readers of the Bible might be inspired to gain an understanding about Melchizedek. Verse 4 says, *"Now observe how great this man was to whom Abraham, the patriarch, gave a tenth of the choicest spoils."* And Verse 7 says, *"But without any dispute the lesser is blessed by the greater."* What does this mean?

Genesis 14:19-20 says, *"He blessed him and said, 'Blessed be Abram of God Most High, Possessor of heaven and earth; and blessed be God Most High, who has delivered your enemies into your hand.' He gave him a tenth of all."*

Melchizedek blessed Abram and Abram gave Melchizedek one tenth of what he had gained. While mentioning this scene, in Hebrews chapter 7 it says "the lesser is blessed by the greater." In other words, the greater blesses the lesser.

Abram would become the Father of Faith and in the Old Testament times those who are saved went to his side (Luke 16:23). Also, he was such a perfect man, even to be worthy to be called a friend of God. Considering these facts about Abraham, who among human beings could say he is higher than Abraham?

Then, who is this Melchizedek? Moreover, consider the fact that Abram gave Melchizedek his one tenth, which is supposed to be given to God. The commandment about 'tithe' had not yet been given in the Law at that time, but Abram was moved in his heart to give the tithe to Melchizedek. This means Abram knew exactly who this Melchizedek was.

Hebrews 7:3 says, *"Without father, without mother, without genealogy, having neither beginning of days nor end of life, but made like the Son of God, he remains a priest perpetually."*

Who among human beings, the creatures, is 'without father, without mother, without genealogy, having neither beginning of days nor end of life'? Hebrews 7:24 says, *"...but Jesus, on the other hand, because He continues forever, holds His priesthood permanently.*" It says the priesthood of Jesus would last forever. And Hebrews 10:21 says, *"…and since we have a great priest over the house of God,"* which means Jesus is the great priest over the house of God.

But Melchizedek is also a perpetual priest and he is like the Son of God. There is a reason why the writer of the book of Hebrews said Melchizedek was like the Son of God.

If he clearly explained about the Holy Spirit to those who did not have sufficient spiritual knowledge, they would have had many misunderstandings. Therefore, he did not clearly explain but just wrote Melchizedek was 'like the Son of God'.

But because Paul knew about Melchizedek clearly, he wrote in Hebrews 1:6, *"And when He again brings the firstborn into the world, He says, 'And let all the angels of God worship Him.'"* He mentioned that the Lord Jesus is the firstborn.

The literal meaning of the word Melchizedek is, "My king is zedek" but the spiritual meaning is "one of the divided ones". It means one of the 'God the Son' and 'God the Holy Spirit' who were begotten by God the Father.

In the Old Testament times, God the Father Himself led and guided the history of mankind, but it doesn't mean the Lord and the Holy Spirit didn't do anything during that time. In particular, the Holy Spirit actively worked as the Spirit to fulfill the will of God the Father and help with His ministry.

One of the works that the Holy Spirit did was to appear as Melchizedek and to bless Abram.

Melchizedek, King of righteousness and King of peace

Hebrews 7:2 says, *"...to whom also Abraham apportioned a tenth part of all the spoils, was first of all, by the translation of his name, king of righteousness, and then also king of Salem, which is king of peace."* Why is it that the Holy Spirit is called King of righteousness and King of peace?

Once we accept Jesus Christ as our personal Savior and receive the gift of the Holy Spirit, from this time on the Holy Spirit in our heart leads us to understand about sin, righteousness, and judgment. He helps us discern between the truth and untruth, righteousness and unrighteousness, and sins and evil, so that we can go into righteousness and goodness. Also, because the Holy Spirit searches even the deep things of God, He teaches us what righteousness in the sight of God is (1 Corinthians 2:10). It is the ministry of the Holy Spirit to help us come forth to perfect righteousness. This is the reason He is called the King of righteousness.

Also, one of the most significant changes that take place in our heart after we receive the gift of the Holy Spirit is the peace in mind. We were sinners and were destined to fall into

Hell. But by repentance we have been forgiven of sins and have become God's children. Now we can go to Heaven. And, the sign that shows that we can go to Heaven is receiving the gift of the Holy Spirit. Once we receive the Holy Spirit, we are acknowledged as God's children who can go to Heaven, and naturally peace comes into our hearts.

Also, when the children of God who have received the Holy Spirit obey the guidance of the Holy Spirit in their lives, they can enjoy the peace that the world cannot give. Therefore, the Holy Spirit is the King of peace.

By giving to Melchizedek one tenth of what he had gained, Abram acknowledged the identity of Melchizedek. At the same time, it was to acknowledge that everything that belonged to him came from God the Creator alone.

The tithe had not yet been mandated in the Law. Abram did not learn about it from anybody. And yet, Abram was moved in his heart and gave his tithe before God. God moved his heart to do so in order to give him the greater blessing; namely, to establish him as the Father of Faith.

Abraham

Chapter 4

The Righteousness of Faith and God's Promise

The promise of the blessing of descendants
A burnt offering with blemish-free sacrifice
Showing the future through a dream
From the river of Egypt as far as the great river, the river Euphrates

1. The promise for the blessing of descendants

> *"After these things the word of the LORD came to Abram in a vision, saying, 'Do not fear, Abram, I am a shield to you; your reward shall be very great.' Abram said, 'O LORD God, what will You give me, since I am childless, and the heir of my house is Eliezer of Damascus?' And Abram said, 'Since You have given no offspring to me, one born in my house is my heir.' Then behold, the word of the LORD came to him, saying, 'This man will not be your heir; but one who will come forth from your own body, he shall be your heir.' And He took him outside and said, 'Now look toward the heavens, and count the stars, if you are able to count them.' And He said to him, 'So shall your descendants be'"* (15:1-5).

After Abram defeated Chedorlaomer and his allied forces and declined the offer of the king of Sodom, God appeared to him in a vision. God said, "Do not fear, Abram, I am a shield to you; your reward shall be very great."

God is love and He always wants to bless us, but because He is the God of justice at the same time, He works perfectly according to the law of justice. Simply speaking, He lets us reap what we sow. For this reason, before He gives blessings, He first lets us prepare the vessel to receive it.

Abram prepared the vessel while going through trials; he loved and revered God from his heart and believed what God said and obeyed it. That is why he could receive such a promise of blessing.

It is not something difficult to prepare your vessel to receive blessings. God does not require anything of us that is complicated and difficult. He requires the things that we are more than able to do if only we have spiritual faith and sincere willingness to obey.

Of course, the depth of what He asks is different depending on the measure of each one's faith. So, within our own measure of faith, if we just love God with all our heart and believe and obey, God will become our shield and fortress and bless us with amazing things (Proverbs 2:7).

During this communication with God, out of the blue Abram talked about his heir saying, *"O LORD God, what will You give me, since I am childless, and the heir of my house is Eliezer of Damascus?"* And *"Since You have given no offspring to me, one born in my house is my heir."*

It tells us how precisely Abram understood the heart of God. What does this mean? God had once told Abram in Genesis 13:16, *"I will make your descendants as the dust of the earth."* So, was it because Abram forgot about this promise of God that he said that Eliezer of Damascus would be his heir? No, it's not like that.

Abram never doubted or forgot anything that God said. Nevertheless, he still said it because he understood exactly why God said, *"I am a shield to you; your reward shall be very great."* Abram knew that God appeared to him to give him the promise about the heir. So, Abram initiated the conversation about his heir feeling that it was the time to receive the promise.

In an allegory, suppose a father promised his son to buy him a new car. After some time, the father felt it was the right time to buy the car. So, the father is about to talk about it. And at this same time the son sensed what his father was going to say and said, "Father, it's OK if I just drive the car I have now."

It's not that the son does not believe his father would buy him a new car. But by saying what he has said, the father will be happier to buy him a new car. Because the son knew exactly what his father was going to say, he received even more certain promise of a new car.

In the same way, for Abram it's not that he did not

believe the words that God had spoken, but by initiating the conversation about his heir, he received the promise of God about his heir.

It was a very certain promise of God. *"This man will not be your heir; but one who will come forth from your own body, he shall be your heir.' And He took him outside and said, 'Now look toward the heavens, and count the stars, if you are able to count them.' And He said to him, 'So shall your descendants be.'"* It was a kind of spiritual conversation that was possible because Abram understood the heart of God precisely.

2. A burnt offering with blemish-free sacrifice

"Then he believed in the LORD; and He reckoned it to him as righteousness. And He said to him, 'I am the LORD who brought you out of Ur of the Chaldeans, to give you this land to possess it.' He said, 'O LORD God, how may I know that I will possess it?' So He said to him, 'Bring Me a three year old heifer, and a three year old female goat, and a three year old ram, and a turtledove, and a young pigeon.' Then he brought all these to Him and cut them in two, and laid each half opposite the other; but he did not cut the birds. The birds of prey came down upon the carcasses, and Abram drove them away" **(15:6-11).**

The promised seed, Abram's heir was not born right after he received the promise of God. A while later Ishmael was born of Hagar, Sarai's maid, but he was not the promised seed. Abram was 86 years old at that time, and it took 14 long years for Isaac, the promised seed, to be born. He was born when Abram was 100.

As in this case, it took a long time for the promise of God to be fulfilled. And for Abram, the heir was not born for a long time even after the promise of God had been given. And yet he did not doubt at all but only believed in God's promise.

That is why verse 6 says, *"Then he believed in the LORD; and He reckoned it to him as righteousness."* About this, Romans 4:13 says, *"For the promise to Abraham or to his descendants that he would be heir of the world was not through the Law, but through the righteousness of faith."*

Righteousness of faith is to look forward to the result with the eyes of faith by relying on the Word of God and by not looking at the reality. It is to rely on the Word and not on our own thoughts or ability.

After God gave Abram the word of promise, Abram by relying on the Word of God accomplished the righteousness of faith with which he could look forward to the fruition of the promise and not the current situation. And until this righteousness of faith was actually revealed through Isaac, he never doubted or changed his mind.

If God says something and shows us the fulfillment right away, who wouldn't believe God? But because some things are revealed right away while some others are not, God can measure each one's righteousness of faith. He allows some tests to see whether we depend on the Word of God or not. And, when the measure that God requires is fulfilled, the answer will be given to us.

God does not want the righteousness of men which changes and betrays following their own benefits. He wants the righteousness of faith that never changes forever. He requires of us the faith with which we look at the fruit to be borne and not the current situation. Thus, when we show this kind of faith, God will also trust us. Abram established this kind of trust with God, and God acknowledged his righteousness as faith.

After acknowledging Abram's righteousness of faith, God said, *"I am the LORD who brought you out of Ur of the Chaldeans, to give you this land to possess it."* Abram replied, *"O LORD God, how may I know that I will possess it?"*

This was not that Abram asked for the confirmation of God because he could not believe God's Word. It was to firmly establish the covenant between God and him.

For example, sometimes a man and a woman who love each other exchange some kind of symbol of love. The symbol itself does not contain the love, but they can remember and feel each other's love seeing that symbol. Love comes from the heart, but they still exchange a symbol that confirms their love.

Abram believed the Word of God from the depth of his heart, but he wanted to reconfirm through the symbol that the promise of God cannot disappear or be taken away by anybody. It is very different from testing God because of unbelief.

If Abram sought a symbol because he did not believe God's Word, God wouldn't have reckoned it to him as righteousness. But Abram did not ask for a sign with doubt. For this reason God had Abram prepare a sacrifice in order to show him the confirmation.

God told him to prepare a three year old heifer, and a three year old female goat, and a three year old ram, and a turtledove, and a young pigeon. These sacrifices represent all the possessions of Abram. It means he was giving all that he had to God.

Three years symbolize being spotless. Heifer, female goat, and ram each represent 'produce'. It means Abram will take the land given by God and multiply in God's blessings.

Cutting them in two carries the meaning that the promise between God and Abram is very accurate. Cutting directly into halves symbolizes that God's promise does not sway to the left or right at all. It also means the covenant between God and Abram was mutual and without an error.

By the way he did not cut the birds. It means there is hierarchy between God and Abram. God and Abram are not equal. Abram is supposed to serve God, and this order must be strictly kept. Not cutting the birds and laying them as a whole means that everything came from God.

When the birds of prey came down upon the carcasses, Abram drove them away. This means nobody can break the covenant made between God and Abram. Birds of prey are detestable (Leviticus 11:13), and them coming down upon the sacrifices could mean 'disturbance of the enemy devil and Satan'. By driving away the birds of prey, Abram made sure nobody could hinder with God's covenant.

Abram did not consider he had done all his duties just by setting the sacrifices before God. Genesis 15:17 says, *"It came about when the sun had set, that it was very dark, and behold, there appeared a smoking oven and a flaming torch which passed between these pieces."* He kept the sacrifices being on the alert until God Himself sent down fire and took the aroma of the sacrifices.

This attitude is also what we need when we want to receive answers to prayers today. Even though we have done everything we are supposed to do to receive an answer, the enemy devil and Satan will not just keep quiet until we receive the answer. Therefore, just as Abram drove away the birds of prey, we also have to be on the alert and drive away the disturbance of the enemy devil and Satan until the answer is actually given. It means we shouldn't be at ease but always pray, being on the alert.

3. Showing the future through a dream

> *"Now when the sun was going down, a deep sleep fell upon Abram; and behold, terror and great darkness fell upon him. God said to Abram, 'Know for certain that your descendants will be strangers in a land that is not theirs, where they will be enslaved and oppressed four hundred years. But I will also judge the nation whom they will serve, and afterward they will come out with many possessions. As for you, you shall go to your fathers in peace; you will be buried at a good old age. Then in the fourth generation they will return here, for the iniquity of the Amorite is not yet complete'"* (15:12-16).

When the sun was going down, a deep sleep fell upon Abram. Darkness fell upon him and he became afraid. 'Deep sleep' means that God was showing Abram a dream. God showed him what would happen to his descendants in future. It was not that their way was not going to be very smooth. It says, "darkness fell upon him" because it was not something bright and peaceful.

Although it was a dream, Abram felt it was real. He was afraid seeing the scene unfold before his eyes. He became fearful the moment he came to know that many hardships would follow his descendants just as we are able to sense from the word 'darkness'. We can see from the history of Israel how hard the road was for the descendants of Abraham until they came into faith having Abraham as their signpost, after he was established as the Father of Faith.

God let Abram know even the details of the things that would take place with his descendants.

God said to Abram, *"Know for certain that your descendants will be strangers in a land that is not theirs, where they will be enslaved and oppressed four hundred years. But I will also judge the nation whom they will serve, and afterward they will come out with many possessions."* This passage is about the fact that the sons of Israel would be enslaved in Egypt for 400 years and then come out of there.

From this passage we can understand that all the proceedings in the history—Joseph being sold into Egypt as a slave and becoming the prime minister, Jacob's family moving into Egypt and later becoming enslaved, and then coming out from there under the leadership of Moses—were not done by any man's power or plan but within the providence and plan of God. Namely, it was not just that Egypt became strong and they enslaved the sons of Israel, but it was only the providence of God to make the sons of Israel into a powerful nation in a very short time.

God even gave Abram the precise numbers and details of what the future held and fulfilled them as He had spoken.

Also God said to Abram, *"As for you, you shall go to your fathers in peace; you will be buried at a good old age."* After he received the calling of God, Abram became such a perfect and blameless person that he could be acknowledged by God as the Father of Faith and the friend of God. So, even in comparison with Elijah and Enoch, Abram was also qualified to be lifted up alive and go to the side of God. However, he faced his death on this earth. It was God's plan, too.

When people die on this earth, those who are saved initially go to the Upper Grave and those who are not saved to the Lower Grave. Abraham stayed in the Upper Grave and accepted the saved souls until Jesus came to this earth, fulfilled His duty as the Savior and resurrected.

Luke 16:22 says, *"Now the poor man died and was carried away by the angels to Abraham's bosom; and the rich man also died and was buried."* It says the poor man Lazarus was saved and went to Abraham's bosom.

Why does it say Abraham's bosom and not the Lord's? It's because until Jesus became the Savior the standard against which people's faith was measured was Abraham, the Father of Faith. But after Jesus became the Savior, the souls go to the Lord's bosom and not Abraham's because the standard of salvation is now Jesus Christ.

Of course, those who were saved before Jesus came to this earth as the Savior still have to be saved in the name of Jesus Christ. In the Old Testament times, people were saved by their deeds of keeping the Law, and these people are given the chance to accept Jesus Christ. It is so that they can be justified by faith and receive salvation according to the law of the spiritual realm.

1 Peter 3:19 says, *"…in which also He [Jesus Christ] went and made proclamation to the spirits now in prison."* Here, the prison refers to the Upper Grave. After He died on the cross, Jesus went down to the Upper Grave for a moment and preached the gospel there. There were souls who were eligible to be saved among those who had died without knowing Jesus Christ. Jesus Christ went there to give these souls a chance to accept Him as their Savior.

Until the way of salvation through Jesus Christ was completed, Abraham remained in the Upper Grave and took care of the saved souls. For this reason Abraham had to go through the process of physical death on this earth. However, Abraham's end was very peaceful. Because he was greatly loved by God, not only all his life's journey but also his last moment was very peaceful.

God also let Abram know that after the enslavement in Egypt his descendants would eventually come back to the land of Canaan in four generations. How would this happen then?

It says 'four generations'. The first generation is the sons of Jacob that moved to Egypt, and the fourth generation would be the people that actually experienced the Exodus. For example, if we consider the genealogy of Moses, Jacob's third son Levi is the first generation, his son Kohath is the second generation, Kohath's son Amram is the third, and Amram's sons Aaron and Moses are the fourth.

So, exactly in the fourth generation after Jacob's sons moved from Canaan to Egypt, their descendants returned to Canaan.

While saying that Abram's descendants would come back in four generations, God said, *"...for the iniquity of the Amorite is not yet complete."*

The 'four generations' was the time for the sons of Israel to increase their faith to be able to go into the land of Canaan. And for the people that lived in the land of Canaan during that time, it was time given by God's mercy for them to repent and turn from their ways.

God does not indiscriminately destroy the Gentiles. God's justice applies to them, too. For this reason God did not let the sons of Israel conquer the land of Canaan immediately. God was patient with the Canaanites until their evil went beyond the limit of punishment according to justice, giving them more chances of repentance.

Of course, the 70 people of Jacob's family could not conquer the Canaan Land. So, it was also for the time that God gave for the sons of Israel to form a big and strong nation. In a spiritual sense, it was not yet the time for God to destroy the people living in the land of Canaan at that time.

In this justice and love of God, a chance was given for the Amorites to repent. But rather than repenting and turning from their ways, they just piled more evil upon evil. After four generations, their evil reached the limit of punishment. Finally, God punished them through the sons of Israel. It was done by the Israelites' conquering of the land of Canaan.

For the sons of Israel, the conquest was a blessing for them to take the Promised Land by faith. At the same time, for the Gentile people living in the land of Canaan at that time, it was a process of punishment for their sins and evil.

God always works with goodness and within the rules of justice. He does not unconditionally bless or protect His children. Of course, if the enemy devil and Satan have nothing to accuse them of, then they won't face any calamities (Proverbs 26:2). Therefore, if there is any problem, we should understand that there must be a reason, find it, and repent before God.

Also, God does not punish us right away even though we have committed iniquity. As in the case of Amorites, He gives us chances again and again so we can realize our faults and turn from our ways. But, if we don't, God allows the accusations of the enemy devil to take place in trials. But this is also God's love. It is so that we can realize ourselves and turn from our wrong ways.

4. From the river of Egypt as far as the great river, the river Euphrates

"It came about when the sun had set, that it was very dark, and behold, there appeared a smoking oven and a flaming torch which passed between these pieces. On that day the LORD made a covenant with Abram, saying, 'To your descendants I have given this land, from the river of Egypt as far as the great river, the river Euphrates: the Kenite and the Kenizzite and the Kadmonite and the Hittite and the Perizzite and the Rephaim and the Amorite and the Canaanite and the Girgashite and the Jebusite'" (15:17-21).

When the sun had set and it was dark, Abram saw a smoking

oven and a flaming torch which passed between these pieces. This was the sign that God accepted Abram's offering as an extremely pleasant aroma.

Depending on what kinds of faith and effort we have when we give offerings to Him and follow His will, God lets us experience His grace.

On the day God established His covenant with Abram, He said the borders of the land which would be given to his descendants was from the river of Egypt as far as the great river, the river Euphrates. It was reconfirmation of His promise that he had had given to Abram before, saying, *"Now lift up your eyes and look from the place where you are, northward and southward and eastward and westward; for all the land which you see, I will give it to you and to your descendants forever."*

God explained how much Abram and his descendants would prevail in the future. In reality, Abram did not have any children, and there were many strong nations that Abram could not overcome. In this situation, God gave Abram such a great promise, and Abram believed Him.

Because Abram accepted the word of God with faith and without any doubt, the word of promise was fulfilled when the time came. By mentioning the land that Abram's descendants would take and the peoples that were living in it currently, God more specifically informed Abram of the area and borders of the land that He would give.

The peoples that lived in that land were the Kenite, Kenizzite, Kadmonite, Hittite, Perizzite, Rephaim, Amorite, Canaanite, Girgashite, and Jebusite.

Each of those Gentile peoples had already taken the land of Canaan by their own power. Therefore, it was not possible to conquer the land with only human power. It was impossible without the help of God. In order to drive out these Gentiles and take the land given by God, God's power was a must. And to bring down His power, faith is absolutely necessary. But until the descendants of Abram came to have faith, they needed time.

As we can see in the history of conquering the land of Canaan, they crossed the Jordan River, destroyed the city of Jericho, and conquered each of the peoples that lived in the land of Canaan. It was only possible through faith.

Therefore, God had to allow the sons of Israel to be under slavery in Egypt for 400 years and the 40 years of wandering in the wilderness, in order to make them a powerful and great nation and to increase their faith that was needed to conquer the land of Canaan.

In Addition 3

Difference between Visions in Old and New Testaments

There are scenes in which Abram communicated with God in visions. The visions in the Old Testament are slightly different from those in the New Testament. A vision is a phenomenon that takes place when God opens a gate to the spiritual realm in the physical space and an individual goes into that spiritual space.

Also, God lets the individual's spiritual eyes and ears open so he can see and hear spiritual things. In this sense visions in both Old and New Testaments are similar. But the difference comes from the area of the spiritual space that is used when God lets people see spiritual things.

On the one hand, visions in the Old Testament use narrower spiritual space than those in the New Testament. So, rather than letting the individual see or feel a lot of things, it was usually a kind of conversation through voice. A spiritual space was unfolded in the physical space and it was surrounded by light. Then, the voice was heard from within this light.

Here, anything surrounded by the light or the voice coming out from the light could not be seen or heard by anybody else but the individual who was seeing the vision. So, when others see this person seeing the vision, they will feel that the person looks like he is praying, but to some extent they can feel that he is seeing a vision.

On the other hand, the visions in the New Testament use a broader spiritual space. God lets the individual feel spiritual things as if he is actually seeing and touching those things firsthand. God opens the spiritual space more broadly so the individual can see many shapes of the things from many different angles.

In the case of John the apostle who wrote the book of Revelations, he saw many things in visions with his spiritual eyes opened. In these visions in the New Testament, the individual feels like he is watching a movie or as if he himself was in the scene. When seeing a vision, sometimes we can just see a particular scene, and at other times we receive the interpretation of the scene at the same time through the inspiration of the Holy Spirit.

Also, because the visions in the New Testament use broader

spiritual space, people who have seen the same vision might tell a slightly different story depending on the direction or the angle they had seeing the vision.

This is the reason why, when people have seen the same vision, the general descriptions are the same, but they might tell slightly different things in the specifics. They might have seen what others haven't or vice versa.

In sum, the visions in the Old Testament and the New Testament are basically similar, but they are different in utilizing the spiritual space. But using the narrower spiritual space in the Old Testament does not mean it is at a spiritually lower level. God shows different kinds of visions according to what He wants us to know.

Visions in the Old Testament are more personal and intimate. It might become a passageway for the people to experience something spiritually deeper. It's because usually it accompanies conversational communication. In visions in the New Testament, a particular scene is shown and the interpretation is given through inspiration while the visions in the Old Testament, a scene is shown and an explanation is given in voice to the spiritual ear that has been opened.

For this reason, we can often see in the Bible that when God let His people know of future things or deep spiritual secrets, He usually worked through the type of visions given in the Old

Testament (Daniel 7:1-2, 15-16, 9:21; Ezekiel 1:1, 1:28).

Therefore, we should be able to understand the similarities and differences between the visions in the Old Testament and the New Testament, and that God works with the most appropriate methods for each occasion.

Abraham

Chapter 5

Hagar's Conception and the Birth of Ishmael

- Sarai gives her maid Hagar as a concubine
- Solving the conflict caused by Hagar's conception of Ishmael
- Hagar meets a God who sees
- Abram begets Ishmael at age 86

1. Sarai gives her maid Hagar as a concubine

"Now Sarai, Abram's wife had borne him no children, and she had an Egyptian maid whose name was Hagar. So Sarai said to Abram, 'Now behold, the LORD has prevented me from bearing children. Please go in to my maid; perhaps I will obtain children through her.' And Abram listened to the voice of Sarai. After Abram had lived ten years in the land of Canaan, Abram's wife Sarai took Hagar the Egyptian, her maid, and gave her to her husband Abram as his wife" (16:1-3).

Sarai was over 70 but did not have a child. She wanted to have a child and demanded her husband Abram to take her maid Hagar as a concubine. Her own desire preceded relying on God.

Sarai experienced the works of God together with Abram and thus she knew about God. However, unlike Abram her experiences did not turn into faith with which she could believe God from her heart. Her experiences just became her knowledge and not true faith in God.

The same can be applied today. Even though people might have seen, heard about and experienced works of God, each one's faith grows at a different pace. The faith of some believers increases very much while that of other believers does not grow up at all. For still others, their faith might even backslide.

Where does this difference come from? It depends on how much each one demolishes their own thoughts and theories and circumcises their heart after experiencing the works of God. If we only consider God's works to be great and store them in our minds as just knowledge, those works cannot become our faith no matter how many times we see them manifested.

We can see that Sarai's faith is faith only as knowledge from her words. She said, *"Now behold, the LORD has prevented me from bearing children. Please go in to my maid; perhaps I will obtain children through her."* She spoke as if it was God's will that she could not bear a child, thereby putting the blame on God.

Her words tell us she just decides everything with her own thoughts and insists on her opinions. She said she would get a child even if it had to be by giving her maid to her husband. It was such an important thing, and yet she neither asked God

His will nor did she consult her husband. She just concluded that she could not have a baby because God wouldn't allow it, and she just informed Abram of her plan.

If Sarai believed in God who was with Abram, what should she have done in a situation where she couldn't have a child?

She should have discussed the matter with her husband in order to realize the will of God. Also, she should have talked about their future plans with her husband. However, she presumptuously thought she understood God and decided on her own what to do next. Then, she just informed Abram of her plan. This was not in accordance with physical order not to mention spiritual order. She just decided everything and informed her husband of her decision without discussing it with him.

Now let's think about the spiritual order here. Abram knows the will of God better than anybody else and obviously she should have consulted with him to know the will of God. Through the trial of his wife being taken away, Abram thoroughly realized how foolish it is to use the thoughts and methods of men before God and what the consequences could be. But Sarai did not learn from the lessons she had, and she is making the same kind of mistake again here.

Right from the beginning Sarai decided everything at her

discretion and carried out her plans. Her plans were neither God's will nor that of Abram. Even in this situation, Abram did not mention any of the will of God that he had realized nor did he try to reason with her to make her wait a little longer. He just listened and accepted her request. Why did he do it?

Here, we can see the differences in the personalities of Abram and Sarai. Considering the actions of Sarai, we can infer that she always insisted on her own thoughts and opinions.

Abram knew her personality well. He knew that she wouldn't change her mind about her decision, even if he did not want to take Hagar. Sarai was the kind of person who would just insist on doing what she wanted no matter how much Abram might try to reason with her.

On the contrary, as we can see from the case where he yielded to his nephew Lot first, Abram always desired to pursue peace with everybody and just listen to other people. He just wanted to follow others' opinions first unless it was sin to do so. Even though he was right, he just wanted to go along with others' opinions.

Because Abram had borne this fruit of peace, he just followed Sarai's will in this matter. He wouldn't follow his own desire or try to serve his interest. Knowing Sarai's personality, he just tried to do what she wanted him to do.

Of course, if it was against the will of God and if it was not allowed by God, Abram wouldn't have listened to Sarai. But because listening to Sarai's suggestion and getting Ishmael was also in the will of God in the grand plan of human cultivation, God did not stop it from happening.

Saying, *"After Abram had lived ten years in the land of Canaan,"* means everything was stable. Abram was affluent and things were peaceful. Now he forgot about the war he fought and he really settled in the land, living a comfortable life. It was this time when this incident with Hagar took place.

When they were going through difficulties Sarai did not have peace of mind and she did not care so much about the fact that she could not have a child. But since everything was stable and settled, the problem of an heir that had been buried now resurfaced. So, within her own thoughts Sarai came up with the idea of giving her maid to her husband.

2. Solving the conflict caused by Hagar's conception of Ishmael

"He went in to Hagar, and she conceived; and when she saw that she had conceived, her mistress was despised in her sight. And Sarai said to Abram, 'May the wrong done me be upon you. I gave my maid into your arms, but when she saw that she had conceived, I was despised in her sight. May the LORD judge between you and

me.' But Abram said to Sarai, 'Behold, your maid is in your power; do to her what is good in your sight.' So Sarai treated her harshly, and she fled from her presence" (16:4-6)

Sarai had never thought Hagar's child would pose any problem for her. She simply thought Hagar was under control because she was merely her maid. But when Hagar became pregnant conflict arose.

Hagar came to know about God through her master Abram, but she did not believe in Him nor was she changed by the truth. So, the moment she realized she became pregnant, the evil in her heart was revealed as despising her mistress. She was arrogant and ungrateful.

She was just a maid and it was by her mistress Sarai's grace that she could become pregnant with Abram's child. Of course, Sarai did not do what she did with good intention, but from Hagar's point of view, she was certainly shown grace. Furthermore, there wasn't any immediate change of her status just because she was pregnant, and yet she despised her mistress. It clearly shows what kind of heart she had.

Through this incident Sarai's evil also surfaced. She said to Abram, *"May the wrong done me be upon you."* It was Sarai who planned the whole thing in the first place. But when she came to suffer because of her plan, she was putting the blame on Abram. She did what she did without even discussing the matter with her husband, and yet she was trying to hold her husband responsible.

She also thought she showed mercy and grace to Hagar. So, she resented Hagar as she began to despise her. Moreover, she acted as though she was the victim in the situation, mentioning the name of God saying, *"May the LORD judge between you and me."*

Abram replied, *"Behold, your maid is in your power; do to her what is good in your sight."* So Sarai persecuted Hagar and Hagar ran away.

While going through such ugly events, Sarai should have looked back on herself, thinking, "What did I do? Did I do something against the will of God?" But she just put the blame on others. When we face unfavorable results due to our fault, we should look back on ourselves humbly before God and realize what went wrong. This way we can realize ourselves through the mistake and make the best out of it by changing ourselves.

Now, why did Abram just let Sarai deal with Hagar as she saw fit so that Hagar would run away? Since Hagar was pregnant with his child, could Abram not have persuaded Sarai to protect Hagar?

He could have, but he just relied on God in everything and did not utilize any human methods. As the head of the family

Abram could have commanded or talked Sarai out of doing anything bad to Hagar. But it would've been merely human thoughts and methods.

Suppose the problem seemed to have been resolved through Abram's intervention, which would've been a human method. But both of the women would still have hard feelings against and hated each other. It couldn't be solved just by telling Sarai or Hagar to bear with each other.

Knowing this situation very well, Abram just committed the matter into God's hands. He did not give orders with his authority as the head of the family, but he just acted following the natural course of things so that God could solve everything.

The natural course was that Sarai had authority over Hagar because Hagar was Sarai's maid. The immediate outcome was that Hagar had to run away from Sarai and into the wilderness. Outwardly it seems the problem got more complicated, but in a spiritual sense, this was the beginning of solving the problem.

3. Hagar meets a God who sees

"Now the angel of the LORD found her by a spring of water in the wilderness, by the spring on the way to Shur. He said, 'Hagar, Sarai's maid, where have you come from and where are you going?' And she said, 'I am fleeing from the presence of my

mistress Sarai.' Then the angel of the LORD said to her, 'Return to your mistress, and submit yourself to her authority.' Moreover, the angel of the LORD said to her, 'I will greatly multiply your descendants so that they will be too many to count.' The angel of the LORD said to her further, 'Behold, you are with child, and you will bear a son; and you shall call his name Ishmael, because the LORD has given heed to your affliction'" (16:7-11).

After Hagar ran into the wilderness, the angel of the LORD appeared to her and said, *"Hagar, Sarai's maid, where have you come from and where are you going?"* It was to remind her of the fact that she was just a maid. And he told Hagar to 'return to her mistress and submit herself to her authority'. What if Abram had told Hagar to obey Sarai unconditionally? Hagar wouldn't have listened to him. She could have also had hard feelings against Abram for saying that.

But as the angel of the LORD commanded her to do so, she had to obey. And the angel of God did not just command her to submit to Sarai's authority. He gave the word of blessing to her at the same time, about the child she would give birth to. If the angel told her to just return and submit, she must have suffered very much thinking, 'How will I be able to endure all the hardships?' But the word of blessing was given: "I will greatly multiply your descendants so that they will be too many to count." And because of this Hagar could obey with hope.

Sarai was also taken aback when Hagar ran away. She was also sorry for Abram. She may have thought, 'Were my actions too much? She is carrying my husband's child after all, and what if something goes wrong and something happens to her?' She finally thought about her previous actions. So, if Hagar came back, she wouldn't persecute her as she had done previously.

As Abram left everything to God following the natural course of things, God caused everything to work together for good. God considered the heart of Abram, whom He loved.

How heartbroken Abram would have been if the conflict between Sarai and Hagar had only heightened? So, considering Abram, God led them in a way that everything could be resolved in peace.

Even today, while doing different kinds of work, there are people who insist on their own opinions and methods or who try to solve the problem with their authority rather than following the natural course of things. In so doing, they hurt the feelings of other people. Peace will eventually be broken and the things won't go well.

Those who are wise will just commit everything into God's hands like Abram did. Then, He will cause all things to work together for good.

4. Abram begets Ishmael at age 86

"'He will be a wild donkey of a man, his hand will be against everyone, and everyone's hand will be against him; and he will live to the east of all his brothers.' Then she called the name of the LORD who spoke to her, 'You are a God who sees'; for she said, 'Have I even remained alive here after seeing Him?' Therefore the well was called Beer-lahai-roi; behold, it is between Kadesh and Bered. So Hagar bore Abram a son; and Abram called the name of his son, whom Hagar bore, Ishmael. Abram was eighty-six years old when Hagar bore Ishmael to him" (16:12-16).

God gave a prophetic message about Ishmael who was going to be born through Hagar. It is said, *"He will be a wild donkey of a man."* It means he will work his way through harsh environments. It means his life will not be an easygoing life, and he will have to pioneer through difficult things to get the land and the basis of life for himself.

As said, *"His hand will be against everyone, and everyone's hand will be against him,"* he will sometimes have to attack other races or be attacked by them. It was said, *"He will live to the east of all his brothers"* meaning God had clearly drawn a line for his settlement.

Ishmael was not the legitimate heir who would continue the orthodox genealogy. Therefore, he could not dwell with

Isaac, the promised seed, and enjoy God's blessing together. God showed mercy to Ishmael considering Abram, but still he was not the authentic seed of blessing. For this reason God gave him a separate area which was far from the land He had promised, so that he could make a living for himself.

After she received the word of promise from the angel of the LORD when she ran away into the wilderness away from Sarai's persecutions, Hagar called the name of God, 'a God who sees'. It was because she felt the hands of God who searches all her circumstances and takes care of her son, even though she was just a maid. After she came to know about the God who sees, she began to change into a person who believed and served Him.

What we have to realize here is that God showed mercy to Hagar and her son Ishmael in consideration of Abram. 'Abram getting Ishmael through Hagar' was not God's idea but a human idea in the first place. And yet, God still gave a word of promise to Ishmael considering the righteous man Abram so that all things would work out peacefully.

Chapter 6

God's Eternal Covenant and the Sign of Circumcision

Walk before Me and be blameless

You will be the father of a multitude of nations

The circumcision for the fulfillment of covenant

The prophecy on Isaac's birth

Every man was circumcised

1. Walk before Me and be blameless

"Now when Abram was ninety-nine years old, the LORD appeared to Abram and said to him, 'I am God Almighty; walk before Me, and be blameless'" **(Genesis 17:1).**

God appeared to Abram once again when he became 99. It was to prepare Abram before the fulfillment of the promise that He had given him.

This was a very important event in the history of human cultivation. For this reason God did not send an angel or just speak to him with His voice but appeared before Abram in person.

God said, *"I am God Almighty; walk before Me, and be blameless."* God called him when he was 75 and caused his faith to be increased through various trials and refinements. And yet, once again God told him to be blameless. To become the Father of Faith, he had to be absolutely blameless.

For the patriarchs in the Bible to be used by God and to receive blessings, they had to prepare their vessels and be acknowledged by God. Now, what is the most important thing in preparing the vessel? Just as God said, Abram had to 'walk before Him and be blameless'.

In the Old Testament this verse meant perfection in action. However during the era of the Holy Spirit we receive the Holy Spirit and circumcise our heart. Thus, it includes perfection and holiness not only in action, but of the heart as well. But this does not mean they did not have to circumcise their hearts in the Old Testament times. What God wants of us is the circumcision of heart, whether in the Old or New Testament.

Deuteronomy 30:6 says, *"Moreover the LORD your God will circumcise your heart and the heart of your descendants, to love the LORD your God with all your heart and with all your soul, so that you may live."* When we love God with all our heart, mind and soul, we may live. And loving God with all our heart and all our soul is achieved by the circumcision of heart, namely by casting away evil from heart.

This is the kind of children God wants to gain through the process of human cultivation. God wants to bring such children into Heaven. Abram knew this heart of God very well, and he became blameless not only in his actions, but in his heart as well.

When God said, *"Walk before Me and be blameless,"* He did not just want perfection of outward actions only but the perfection in actions that came out from the heart. Actions are important, but what is more important is the heart. But when we say actions are important in Christian faith, some misunderstand it as being legalistic, which is not something that is desirable. But the Bible always talks about the importance of actions along with the cleanliness of heart.

When Abraham passed the last test of giving his only son Isaac, God blessed him and said, *"...because you have obeyed My voice."*

Concerning this, James 2:21-22 says, *"Was not Abraham our father justified by works when he offered up Isaac his son on the altar? You see that faith was working with his works, and as a result of the works, faith was perfected."*

2. You will be the father of a multitude of nations

> *"'I will establish My covenant between Me and you, and I will multiply you exceedingly.'" Abram fell on his face, and God talked with him, saying, 'As for Me, behold, My covenant is with you, and you will be the father of a multitude of nations. No longer shall your name be called Abram, but your name shall be Abraham; for I will make you the father of a multitude of nations. I will make you*

exceedingly fruitful, and I will make nations of you, and kings will come forth from you. I will establish My covenant between Me and you and your descendants after you throughout their generations for an everlasting covenant, to be God to you and to your descendants after you. I will give to you and to your descendants after you, the land of your sojournings, all the land of Canaan, for an everlasting possession; and I will be their God'" **(Genesis 17:2-8).**

This was the amazing promise of God given to Abram. First, God changed his name saying, *"No longer shall your name be called Abram, but your name shall be Abraham."*

Abraham means the 'father of a multitude of people'. In the passage God said, 'the father of a multitude of nations.' It meant that through Abraham there would be many descendants of faith who would come forth throughout the generations.

God promised that countless descendants would prevail through Abraham, and many kings would also come forth from among them. God continued, *"I will establish My covenant between Me and you and your descendants after you throughout their generations for an everlasting covenant, to be God to you and to your descendants after you. I will give to you and to your descendants after you, the land of your sojournings, all the land of Canaan, for an everlasting possession; and I will be their God."*

This means that, based on the covenant between God and Abraham, God would lead and control everything in the course of human history until the end of the ages. It means even until the end of human cultivation, God will not forsake the sons of Israel but still be their God, because of this covenant with Abraham.

3. The circumcision for the fulfillment of covenant

"God said further to Abraham, 'Now as for you, you shall keep My covenant, you and your descendants after you throughout their generations. This is My covenant, which you shall keep, between Me and you and your descendants after you: every male among you shall be circumcised. And you shall be circumcised in the flesh of your foreskin, and it shall be the sign of the covenant between Me and you. And every male among you who is eight days old shall be circumcised throughout your generations, a servant who is born in the house or who is bought with money from any foreigner, who is not of your descendants. A servant who is born in your house or who is bought with your money shall surely be circumcised; thus shall My covenant be in your flesh for an everlasting covenant. But an uncircumcised male who is not circumcised in the flesh of his foreskin, that person shall be cut off from his people; he has broken My covenant'" **(Genesis 17:9-14).**

While God was giving Abraham His promise, He commanded him to perform the circumcision as a sign to confirm the covenant. He said, *"This is My covenant, which you shall keep, between Me and you and your descendants after you: every male among you shall be circumcised."*

According to this command, God's covenant will be in effect only for those who have been circumcised. Even though God gives us a promise of great blessing, it is of no use as long as we do not receive it with faith. Circumcision was a sign to show this kind of faith.

Circumcision is surgical removal of the foreskin of males. God commanded that they be circumcised when they are eight days old. Since then, all sons of Israel have obeyed this commandment, and they performed circumcision even on the Sabbath (John 7:22-23).

What is the reason God commanded circumcision? God is telling the believers that they have to show their faith through deeds. If we believe in God, there must be the following actions. In this regard, God commanded circumcision as an act to show their faith. Circumcision is a promise of men, showing to God that they will keep the words of God. It is to prove that they believe in God, and at the same time, it is their promise to God that they will live according to God's Word (Galatians 5:3; Romans 2:25-26).

God commanded that even the Gentiles that had been

bought with money must be circumcised. He said, *"And every male among you who is eight days old shall be circumcised throughout your generations, a servant who is born in the house or who is bought with money from any foreigner, who is not of your descendants..."* This symbolizes that salvation is not confined to only the sons of Israel, but among all peoples and nations, anyone who is circumcised, namely anyone who has the covenant established with God, can receive salvation.

Whether sons of Israel or Gentiles, to be circumcised spiritually means they have come into the covenant of God, namely the boundary of salvation. This is not decided just by whether one is circumcised physically or not. It is decided by whether one is in the covenant of God or not.

Salvation can be received only by somebody who has accepted Jesus Christ as his personal Savior, accepted the promise to become a child of God, and lives by the Word of God. Abraham was called the father of a multitude of nations in order to become the father of all believers among all peoples and nations.

God says, *"But an uncircumcised male who is not circumcised in the flesh of his foreskin, that person shall be cut off from his people; he has broken My covenant."* When people have made agreements between them, it cannot be in effect if only one party signs it. In the same way, in the covenant between God and us, both sides have to sign it so that the covenant is put into effect.

And circumcision is the same as signing the covenant from the side of man. Therefore, those who are not circumcised have nothing to do with God, and they will be cut off from God. So then, how is this circumcision supposed to be performed?

Colossians 2:11 says, *"...and in Him you were also circumcised with a circumcision made without hands, in the removal of the body of the flesh by the circumcision of Christ."* Those who believe that Jesus died on the cross for our sins must not live in sins any longer. They have to change through the Word of God. This is how a person is to show the sign of their faith.

Going to church, having titles in the church, or doing voluntary services in the church are only circumcision of the flesh exhibiting outwardly we are Christians. But God wants the circumcision of heart. He considers how much evil we have cast away and how holy we have become through gaining a resemblance to the Lord. This resemblance is how much of a heart of spirit we have that resembles God's heart.

Therefore, we should not consider ourselves Christians just because we love God with words and tongue, but we have to love in deed and truth (1 John 3:18). Namely, we should be able to show that we are citizens of the heavenly kingdom who are saved and true children of God who love Him with the deeds that come out from a truthful heart.

4. The prophecy on Isaac's birth

"Then God said to Abraham, 'As for Sarai your wife, you shall not call her name Sarai, but Sarah shall be her name. I will bless her, and indeed I will give you a son by her. Then I will bless her, and she shall be a mother of nations; kings of peoples will come from her.' Then Abraham fell on his face and laughed, and said in his heart, 'Will a child be born to a man one hundred years old? And will Sarah, who is ninety years old, bear a child?' And Abraham said to God, 'Oh that Ishmael might live before You!' But God said, 'No, but Sarah your wife will bear you a son, and you shall call his name Isaac; and I will establish My covenant with him for an everlasting covenant for his descendants after him. As for Ishmael, I have heard you; behold, I will bless him, and will make him fruitful and will multiply him exceedingly. He shall become the father of twelve princes, and I will make him a great nation. But My covenant I will establish with Isaac, whom Sarah will bear to you at this season next year.' When He finished talking with him, God went up from Abraham" **(Genesis 17:15-22).**

God did not just change Abram's name into Abraham. He

changed the name of Sarai into Sarah, which means 'a mother of nations'. God gave His word of blessing that He would bless Sarah to let her give birth to a son and eventually become a mother of nations, and kings of peoples would come from her.

The reason why Sarah could receive such a great blessing was due to Abraham. Of course, one has to prepare his vessel through his own effort to receive blessings. But sometimes, like in this case of Sarah, one might receive blessings just by being with a righteous man.

When God said Sarah would give birth to a son, Abraham responded in an unexpected way. He fell on his face and laughed, and said in his heart, *'Will a child be born to a man one hundred years old? And will Sarah, who is ninety years old, bear a child?'*

If you interpret this passage literally, you might have a misunderstanding about the reason why Abraham laughed. You might think Abraham laughed because he couldn't believe the word of God or because he was dumbfounded. But that is not the case at all.

As a matter of fact, Abraham thought, *'Will a child be born to a man one hundred years old? And will Sarah, who is ninety years old, bear a child?'* to profess in his heart his trust in the almighty God.

Of course it is impossible by the nature of the law for this old couple to have a baby. Nevertheless, Abraham certainly believed that God would fulfill everything.

About this, Romans 4:18-20 says, *"In hope against hope he believed, so that he might become a father of many nations according to that which had been spoken, 'So shall your descendants be.' Without becoming weak in faith he contemplated his own body, now as good as dead since he was about a hundred years old, and the deadness of Sarah's womb; yet, with respect to the promise of God, he did not waver in unbelief but grew strong in faith, giving glory to God."*

Then, what is the reason Abraham laughed when he heard the Word of God telling him that Sarah would give birth to a son? It was the laughter of joy.

It had been a long time since he had received the promise for a son. But Abraham still believed in the promise. He also knew that Ishmael, whom he begot through Hagar was not the promised seed.

And now, as God changed the name of Sarai and promised him a son, Abraham realized in his heart it was time for the fulfillment of God's promise and laughed with joy.

When Abraham thought, *'Will a child be born to a man one hundred years old? And will Sarah, who is ninety years old, bear a child?'* he didn't mean that it was impossible. It was that he expressed his faith in God that He could do even the impossible.

Verse 18 says, *"And Abraham said to God, 'Oh that Ishmael might live before You!'"* What does this mean, then? People usually interpret it as that Abraham asked God to let Ismael live because he couldn't have a baby due to old age. But it is not correct.

Had Abraham been a person who didn't have any faith, even to openly deny the Word of God, God wouldn't have chosen him in the first place. God would never have given him the promised seed either.

Abraham never doubted the Word of God. He was very certain that he would get the promised son. Therefore, when he said, *"Oh that Ishmael might live before You!"* he meant, "God, please take care of Ishmael, too." If you have children, you might understand the kind of heart Abraham had at this moment.

Even though Ishmael was not the promised seed, he still was a precious son to Abraham. Abraham knew that the authenticity of his genealogy would be kept through the promised seed that would be born later, but it doesn't mean Abraham would just ignore Ishmael.

For this reason, at the moment he was receiving the Word of God about the promised seed, he asked God to take care of Ishmael saying, "God, please take care of Ishmael, too, and not just the promise seed that would be born. Bless Ishmael and let him live before You." This was the prayer out of earnest love of a father toward his son.

So, God said, *"No, but Sarah your wife will bear you a son, and you shall call his name Isaac; and I will establish My covenant with him for an everlasting covenant for his descendants after him."* God told Abraham to name the son who would be born 'Isaac', and that He would establish a covenant with Isaac, which would be an everlasting covenant for his descendants after him.

'No' here does not mean God is rejecting the request of Abraham to take care of Ishmael. It just means that God's covenant will be fulfilled through Isaac whom Sarah would bear, and not through Ishmael. It is that once again God placed emphasis on and explained about the promised seed, Isaac.

After that, concerning Ishmael, God said, *"I have heard you; behold, I will bless him, and will make him fruitful and will multiply him exceedingly. He shall become the father of twelve princes, and I will make him a great nation."*

Although Ishmael was not the promised seed, he still belonged to Abraham, and God opened a way for him and his descendants to multiply and receive blessings. God's promise toward Ishmael that his descendants would be a great nation was fulfilled in the course of human history (Genesis 25:13-

16).

God continued to say, *"But My covenant I will establish with Isaac, whom Sarah will bear to you at this season next year."* God now mentioned the specific time when the promised seed would be born. As He was saying that He would form the chosen people through Isaac and his descendants, He gave even the specific time when Isaac would be born.

After giving the word of blessing to Abraham and establishing a covenant with him, God went up from Abraham. From this conversation between God and Abraham, we can understand how delicately God was guiding Abraham and how faithfully He was fulfilling His promise.

God guided Abraham at every important moment by showing Himself to him or by showing him visions. And Abraham could overcome at each moment by completely trusting and obeying God who was delicate and kind to him.

5. Every man was circumcised

"Then Abraham took Ishmael his son, and all the servants who were born in his house and all who were bought with his money, every male among the men of Abraham's household, and circumcised the flesh of their foreskin in the very same day, as God had said to him. Now Abraham was ninety-nine years old when

he was circumcised in the flesh of his foreskin. And Ishmael his son was thirteen years old when he was circumcised in the flesh of his foreskin. In the very same day Abraham was circumcised, and Ishmael his son. All the men of his household, who were born in the house or bought with money from a foreigner, were circumcised with him" **(Genesis 17:23-27).**

After receiving the promise of God, Abraham showed his trust in God by immediately obeying His Word. Namely, he conducted circumcision on himself, Ishmael, and every man in his household. He carried out the command of God perfectly. He circumcised not just those who were born in his household but also those who had been bought with money. It was a complete obedience to God.

At that time Abraham was 99 years old and Ishmael was 13. Abraham did not postpone the circumcision by giving excuses. He performed the circumcision on many men that day.

If you think about it, it was something very inconvenient and dangerous to circumcise every man in the household on the same day. At least for a couple of days they would suffer the pain and they can't move their bodies freely. If there was any outside attack, they'd be completely defenseless.

So, you might come up with an idea to circumcise a certain portion of men and take turns, or you might consider all the other circumstances and decide a certain day to perform the circumcision. But Abraham did not implement any kind of human thoughts. He just performed the circumcision on every male in his household as soon as God commanded it.

This was how Abraham obeyed the Word of God all the time; namely, he did not utilize his own thoughts but immediately obeyed. That is why he could become the Father of Faith and God's will was fulfilled through him. In view of justice, he was completely qualified to be used as an instrument of God.

"In Your sight, Father,
I tried to show perfect faith,
But sometimes I used my own thoughts.
But Father, because You love me,
You opened all the ways for me.
You guided me and You molded me in every way.

Father, You refine me to perfect me,
And my thanks for You has been stored up,
So that when I see all things,
I do not see them with the eyes of the actualities,
But I see them with the eyes of the Father.
Father, I give You thanks,
For guiding me to have such a heart.

And today, I have with me this wealth,
This honor, this fame,
And this glory of the Father,
So that I am praised by many,
And my son gives me joy, and I give You thanks.

Part 2

Sacrifice and Submission

The second step to become the friend of God

Part 2

Even if God speaks of something that is completely opposite to our way of thinking, we must believe that there is the good will of God in what He said. This is real trust.

Furthermore, if we realize what His good will is, understand the deep part of God's heart, and obey Him, then it means we have reached the level of complete submission.

When Abraham reached this level of submission,
God recognized him as His friend.

Abraham

Chapter 7

"Shall I hide from Abraham what I am about to do?"

- The three persons by the oak of Mamre
- Is anything too difficult for the LORD?
- Revealing the imminent destruction of Sodom and Gomorrah
- The intercession offered with love and in justice

1. The three persons by the oak of Mamre

"Now the LORD appeared to him by the oaks of Mamre, while he was sitting at the tent door in the heat of the day. When he lifted up his eyes and looked, behold, three men were standing opposite him; and when he saw them, he ran from the tent door to meet them and bowed himself to the earth, and said, 'My lord, if now I have found favor in your sight, please do not pass your servant by. Please let a little water be brought and wash your feet, and rest yourselves under the tree; and I will bring a piece of bread, that you may refresh yourselves; after that you may go on, since you have visited your servant.' And they said, 'So do, as you have said.' So Abraham hurried into the tent to Sarah, and said, 'Quickly, prepare three measures of fine flour, knead it and make bread cakes.' Abraham also ran to the herd, and took a tender and choice calf and gave it to the servant, and he hurried to prepare it. He took curds and milk and the calf which he had prepared, and

placed it before them; and he was standing by them under the tree as they ate" (Genesis 18:1-8).

After he settled in Hebron, south of Jerusalem, Abraham met the LORD God once again by the oaks of Mamre. He was sitting at the tent door in the heat of the day and saw three men.

He ran from the tent door to meet them and bowed himself to the earth. He asked them to wash their feet, take a rest under the tree, and take some refreshments before they went on. They accepted this hospitality of Abraham. Here, we can see Abraham was serving them with his utmost humbleness and so much respect for them.

At that time, there weren't so many commercial accommodations where sojourners could stay. Neither were there many residents in the area. So, it was their custom to invite travelers in and show them hospitality. And probably it was something natural for people like Abraham to invite the travelers in and serve them, for he was a very good-hearted person who loved giving to others.

But we can still see that Abraham's actions were not just some hospitality. He ordered his wife Sarah to bring fine flour and bake bread, and he himself ran to the herd, and took a tender and choice calf. Also, he served the guests himself and waited on them himself.

He was such a great and influential man who was rich and

powerful enough to defeat the allied forces. In a spiritual sense he was such a precious person who was loved and attested to by God. And it was this great Abraham who ran towards the travelers, bowed himself before them, invited them to his house and waited on them himself. Furthermore, he called them 'my lord', lowering himself as much as possible.

What is strange is the attitude of these three. In their manner of speaking they spoke to Abraham as if he was their subordinate and they had known each other well when they said, "Where is Sarah your wife?"

Now, who were these men that Abraham served them with his utmost sincerity? We have a clue from the contents of the conversation between them and Abraham.

Verse 13 says, *"And the LORD said to Abraham."* Therefore, one of the three is the LORD God. Then, who were the other two who accompanied the LORD God? In verse 22, we see the LORD God remained there to engage in more conversation with Abraham, and the other two left for Sodom.

Furthermore, in Genesis 19:1 it says, *"Now the two angels came to Sodom in the evening as Lot was sitting in the gate of Sodom. When Lot saw them, he rose to meet them and bowed down with his face to the ground."*

Here, we can infer that the two men that accompanied the LORD God were angels. Also, from the fact that Lot recognized them, we can also see that Lot had met them before. We can also understand that the angels were not ordinary angels since they accompanied the LORD God to this earth. These two angels were the archangels that served God in positions right next to Him.

The three men that appeared before Abraham that day were the LORD God and two archangels that served God. Abraham served them with his utmost humbleness because he recognized them the moment he saw them. Lot, too, recognized these two archangels immediately.

Then, how were Abraham and Lot able to recognize God and the two archangels that appeared in a human form? We can find the answer from the event where Abram met with Melchizedek on his way back home from rescuing his nephew, Lot (Genesis chapter 14). It was God the Holy Spirit who appeared in the image of Melchizedek and met with Abram. It was the same God the Holy Spirit who appeared in the form of a man before Abraham this time also.

Since Abraham had met God the Holy Spirit once before who had appeared as Melchizedek, he was able to recognize Him immediately when He appeared again. Of course, when God the Holy Spirit had appeared the first time, the same two archangels accompanied Him. For this reason Abraham recognized the two archangels this time as well.

Lot also recognized the two archangels, because when the archangels appeared for the first time, God knowing what would come in the future let Lot's spiritual eyes open so he could see them.

Lot had seen the two archangels that were with Melchizedek, so when they came to Sodom this time, he could recognize them right away.

2. Is anything too difficult for the LORD?

"Then they said to him, 'Where is Sarah your wife?' And he said, 'There, in the tent.' He said, 'I will surely return to you at this time next year; and behold, Sarah your wife will have a son.' And Sarah was listening at the tent door, which was behind him. Now Abraham and Sarah were old, advanced in age; Sarah was past childbearing. Sarah laughed to herself, saying, 'After I have become old, shall I have pleasure, my lord being old also?' And the LORD said to Abraham, 'Why did Sarah laugh, saying, 'Shall I indeed bear a child, when I am so old?' 'Is anything too difficult for the LORD? At the appointed time I will return to you, at this time next year, and Sarah will have a son.' Sarah denied it however, saying, 'I did not laugh'; for she was afraid. And He said, 'No, but you did laugh'" **(Genesis 18:9-15).**

The passage reveals the reason why God appeared before Abraham. It was to let him know when Sarah would give birth to the promised heir.

Abraham and Sarah were already old, and Sarah was past childbearing. In this situation, upon hearing God's word, Sarah laughed to herself thinking, *'After I have become old, shall I have pleasure, my lord being old also?'* If we just interpret it literally, we might think it was very similar to the occasion in which Abraham said in Genesis 17:17, *"Will a child be born to a man one hundred years old? And will Sarah, who is ninety years old, bear a child?"* However, the kind of heart that Abraham had at that time was completely different from that of Sarah.

The reason why Abraham laughed at that time was his joy of realizing that the fulfillment of the promise was very near. Also, Abraham's confession was made out of his complete trust in God who could do anything, even the things that men could never do.

But Sarah's words carried different meaning. She just had fleshly thoughts. She doubted the power of the almighty God and revealed her own disbelief. God said to Abraham, *"Why did Sarah laugh, saying, 'Shall I indeed bear a child, when I am so old?' Is anything too difficult for the LORD? At the appointed time I will return to you, at this time next year, and Sarah will have a son."* Once again, God clearly informed him of the time of birth.

Sarah now became afraid of God who knew the depth of her heart and said, *"I did not laugh."* But nobody can deceive God. God said once again, *"No, but you did laugh,"* so Sarah could no longer deny it.

3. Revealing the imminent destruction of Sodom and Gomorrah

"Then the men rose up from there, and looked down toward Sodom; and Abraham was walking with them to send them off. The LORD said, 'Shall I hide from Abraham what I am about to do, since Abraham will surely become a great and mighty nation, and in him all the nations of the earth will be blessed? For I have chosen him, so that he may command his children and his household after him to keep the way of the LORD by doing righteousness and justice, so that the LORD may bring upon Abraham what He has spoken about him.' And the LORD said, 'The outcry of Sodom and Gomorrah is indeed great, and their sin is exceedingly grave. I will go down now, and see if they have done entirely according to its outcry, which has come to Me; and if not, I will know" **(Genesis 18:16-21).**

After the two angels left for Sodom and Gomorrah, God

spoke with Abraham. He said, *"Shall I hide from Abraham what I am about to do,"* and clearly informed Abraham of the things to come.

God trusted Abraham enough to tell him even the secrets. Such a close relationship was not formed overnight. The more Abraham trusted and relied on God by demolishing his fleshly thoughts through trials, the more God trusted Abraham, too.

Building up the trust with God step by step, Abraham finally reached a level of complete trust where he could be called the friend of God.

God gave Abraham a word of promise. God said, *"Since Abraham will surely become a great and mighty nation, and in him all the nations of the earth will be blessed."* God reconfirmed that His covenant would certainly be fulfilled. Furthermore, God also talked about the plans He had in mind regarding the promised seed.

But such promises wouldn't be fulfilled unconditionally. As written, *"For I have chosen him, so that he may command his children and his household after him to keep the way of the LORD by doing righteousness and justice,"* the promise can be fulfilled only through those who keep the way of the LORD.

And it was Abraham who was the most qualified to do so, and for this reason he was chosen. Through the example of Abraham, God wanted to show how one is supposed to obey

God's word in faith, so that people of later generations could follow his example to fulfill the will of God. God's works are fulfilled only through those who obey God's commandments.

After giving Abraham such an important word of promise, God continued to talk about Sodom and Gomorrah. God said, *"The outcry of Sodom and Gomorrah is indeed great, and their sin is exceedingly grave. I will go down now, and see if they have done entirely according to its outcry, which has come to Me; and if not, I will know."* God had three reasons in saying this.

First, it was that He wanted to be very careful and check once again before He made the final decision, even though He knew everything, so that nothing would be against the law of Justice. The punishment that would come upon Sodom and Gomorrah was such a tremendous disaster that it would wipe out everything there. For this reason God wanted to make sure there was no single error.

Second, it was that He wanted Abraham to keep in mind once again what consequences sins would result in and how alarmed the people had to be against sins. God gave an amazing promise of blessing. But for this promise to be fulfilled to the fullest extent, there couldn't be any descendant of Abraham who would follow the way of people of Sodom and Gomorrah.

For this reason, God spoke clearly of the process of the destruction of Sodom and Gomorrah, so that Abraham and his descendants could be on the alert.

Third, by foretelling Abraham about the destruction of Sodom and Gomorrah, God wanted to open a way of salvation for his nephew Lot who was living there.

When Abraham heard about the imminent punishment on Sodom and Gomorrah, who do you think Abraham thought of first? It was Lot whom he had always had concerns about. Since Lot's city, Sodom, was to be destroyed, Abraham prayed even more earnestly thinking about Lot.

Spiritual law dictates we get answers only when we ask. And the prayer of a righteous man offered with love and faith is powerful (James 5:16). Therefore, by informing Abraham of the imminent punishment of Sodom, God let Abraham pray for Lot. It was so that God would answer Abraham's prayer and open a way for Lot to be saved.

God is giving Lot and his family the last chance considering Abraham. This might seem unfair in the view of fleshly men, but it is very just in a spiritual sense. God's justice is completed in love, and that is why such a chance was given.

Sodom and Gomorrah reached a state where they couldn't be forgiven due to their grave sins. And yet, God did not destroy them right away but in an attempt to find a reason not to punish them, He sent the Holy Spirit to look for the reason.

The Three of the Triune God have both divinity and humanity, and the Holy Spirit shows relatively stronger traits of humanity in a sense that He wants to care for people and show compassion to them. That is why God sent the Holy Spirit to have a look at the situation of Sodom and Gomorrah with a relatively more compassionate view, and to show them as much grace as possible.

4. The intercession offered with love and in justice

"Then the men turned away from there and went toward Sodom, while Abraham was still standing before the LORD. Abraham came near and said, 'Will You indeed sweep away the righteous with the wicked? Suppose there are fifty righteous within the city; will You indeed sweep it away and not spare the place for the sake of the fifty righteous who are in it? Far be it from You to do such a thing, to slay the righteous with the wicked, so that the righteous and the wicked are treated alike. Far be it from You! Shall not the Judge of all the earth deal justly?' So the LORD said, 'If I find in Sodom fifty righteous within the city, then I will spare the whole place on their account.' And Abraham replied, 'Now behold, I have ventured to speak to the LORD, although I am but

dust and ashes. Suppose the fifty righteous are lacking five, will You destroy the whole city because of five?' And He said, 'I will not destroy it if I find forty-five there.' He spoke to Him yet again and said, 'Suppose forty are found there?' And He said, 'I will not do it on account of the forty.' Then he said, 'Oh may the LORD not be angry, and I shall speak; suppose thirty are found there?' And He said, 'I will not do it if I find thirty there.' And he said, 'Now behold, I have ventured to speak to the LORD; suppose twenty are found there?' And He said, 'I will not destroy it on account of the twenty.' Then he said, 'Oh may the LORD not be angry, and I shall speak only this once; suppose ten are found there?' And He said, 'I will not destroy it on account of the ten.' As soon as He had finished speaking to Abraham the LORD departed, and Abraham returned to his place" **(Genesis 18:22-33).**

Hearing the news about the imminent punishment on Sodom and Gomorrah, Abraham discreetly asked God, *"Will You indeed sweep away the righteous with the wicked? Suppose there are fifty righteous within the city; will You indeed sweep it away and not spare the place for the sake of the fifty righteous who are in it?"*

Then God said He would forgive if He were to find fifty righteous men. Abraham did not stop there, but continued to ask God to forgive the city for the sake of forty five, forty, thirty, twenty, and eventually as few as ten righteous men. But regretfully, Sodom did not have ten righteous men.

Abraham interceded for Sodom, changing his request five times before God. The reason why he could do this was because he understood the heart of God who wanted to save as many souls as possible.

This heart of God can be vividly seen when He saved the people of Nineveh. Nineveh was the capital city of Assyria and had been giving hard times to Israel. They were so corrupt that their wickedness had gone up to God.

And yet, God did not punish them immediately. He sent Jonah the prophet to give them a chance to repent. As a result, the people of Nineveh repented with humility and with fasting. God forgave them and did not destroy them. God keeps to the standard of justice, but He always acts in love.

Now, what is the reason that God the Holy Spirit is written as the 'LORD God' in Genesis chapter 18?

The history of human cultivation can be generally categorized into three eras. The first is when God the Father Himself governed the history and led the people. The second is when Jesus, God the Son, came down to this earth and ministered. The third is the era during which the Holy Spirit ministers.

In the Old Testament, we can find multiple events where the LORD God ministered. Sometimes He let His voice be heard while at other times He showed visions. He also sent His angels to the people. Of course, even for this moment, everything in human cultivation is governed by God the Father. But during the Old Testament times, He accomplished His word on the frontline.

Later, Jesus, God the Son, came down to this earth to do the ministry as the Savior. And then, when He ascended, He handed over the ministry to the Holy Spirit. From that time on it has been the era of the Holy Spirit that continues until the Lord comes back again to take us.

However, this does not mean that God the Father worked all by Himself during the Old Testament times, and the Lord Jesus and the Holy Spirit did not do any work. Also, the 'era of the Holy Spirit' does not mean that God the Father and the Lord Jesus are just watching the Holy Spirit's ministry.

The Triune God always works together. Therefore, even in the Old Testament times, the Lord and the Holy Spirit helped with the ministry of God the Father. Even in this era of the Holy Spirit today, God the Father and the Lord are actively working, too. It's just that there is a main character for each era, and most ministries are done in the name of the main character.

Therefore, in the Old Testament times, even while the Lord and the Holy Spirit were working, they worked under the name of God the Father. In the same way, in the era of the Holy Spirit, God the Father and the Lord often work in the name of the Holy Spirit.

This is the reason why God the Holy Spirit who came down to punish Sodom and Gomorrah was referred to as the LORD God. It was the Holy Spirit who came down, but He was referred to as the LORD God, because He came on behalf of God the Father.

In Addition 4

What does 'Behold, three men' mean?

About God the Holy Spirit and the two archangels, the Bible does not say Abraham saw God and the angels but just 'three men'. What is the reason? It is so that we can understand the methods and appearances of God when He appeared before Abraham.

There were many ways in which God showed Himself to Abraham. In some cases, He revealed Himself in dreams and visions, while in other cases He spoke with His voice. He once came down in the form of Melchizedek. In the case of Melchizedek, it was that God opened the spiritual space before Abraham who was in the physical realm, so that he could see Him.

In order for us to be able to meet and feel God who is in the spiritual realm, our spiritual eyes and ears must be opened.

Only then can we see God and hear His voice. If our spiritual eyes are not opened, we can never see what is happening in the spiritual realm, even though it is happening right next to us. Perhaps, we can feel in spirit that something is going on.

When God appeared with two archangels to examine Sodom and Gomorrah, it was a completely different case from other cases. In that particular event, God did not just open the spiritual space in the physical space, but He came out to the physical space in person. Though to a limited degree, He put the physical space on Himself to appear in the physical space.

This can be likened to the difference between seeing God on TV and in real life. So, in this case where God came out to the physical space, even those people whose spiritual eyes are not opened can see God, and when they do, they see Him as a person.

Abraham also saw the image of God when He and the two archangels put on the physical space and appeared in the image of human beings. That is why the Bible says he saw three men. But in the case of Abraham, he did not just see them as in the image of men. His spiritual eyes also opened at the same time, so he could see their spiritual images, too. He saw both the images that put on the physical space as well as the original appearance of their spirit.

Then, why did God come down to this earth along with

the two archangels in a human image? It was to see Sodom and Gomorrah in person. Of course, He could have come down in spirit to see those cities, but it was to investigate the sins and wickedness of Sodom and Gomorrah in greater detail.

And because the two archangels appeared in a human form before the people of Sodom and Gomorrah, God could see for Himself more vividly the corruption of those people. If He had just come down in spirit, He wouldn't have been able to feel their evil directly and as vividly. But because He came down in a human image, He could experience it and feel it firsthand.

Chapter 8

The Two Archangels and Lot's Salvation

The arrival and receiving of the two archangels in Sodom

The corrupt Sodomites and the two archangels

The two archangels bring Lot and his family out

God saves Lot in consideration of Abraham

The judgment of fire on Sodom and Gomorrah

Fathers of Moab and Ammon

1. The arrival and receiving of the two archangels in Sodom

"Now the two angels came to Sodom in the evening as Lot was sitting in the gate of Sodom. When Lot saw them, he rose to meet them and bowed down with his face to the ground. And he said, 'Now behold, my lords, please turn aside into your servant's house, and spend the night, and wash your feet; then you may rise early and go on your way.' They said however, 'No, but we shall spend the night in the square.' Yet he urged them strongly, so they turned aside to him and entered his house; and he prepared a feast for them, and baked unleavened bread, and they ate" (19:1-3).

The two archangels that visited Abraham left around noon and arrived at Sodom toward dusk. Sodom was not so far from where Abraham was living.

If the angels moved through the spiritual space or used some power that superseded physical laws, they could have moved in an instant. But the fact that the two archangels arrived at Sodom in the evening means that they followed the physical law completely. More simply put, it means they walked just like any other people.

The reason why they did that was to search everything having the exact same conditions with men. They did not just instantly fly over Sodom and decide judgment, but they actually walked on the land and searched all the circumstances around Sodom.

Lot was sitting in the gate of Sodom, and when he saw them he rose to meet them. Sitting in the gate means that he was very tired of the life there and his heart was empty. About this, 2 Peter 2:7-8 says, *""...and if He rescued righteous Lot, oppressed by the sensual conduct of unprincipled men (for by what he saw and heard that righteous man, while living among them, felt his righteous soul tormented day after day by their lawless deeds)."*

Lot chose the land that looked good in his eyes and settled in Sodom despite the fact that he had learned the truth from Abraham. However, this did not mean his heart was too numb to feel tormented while seeing the lawless deeds being vividly carried out in Sodom.

How oppressed Lot's heart must have been when he saw the Sodomites who were so stained by sins that God's punishment was imminent! Lot was tired of that kind of life there and he felt empty. He had regrets, comparing his current life with the one he had lived with Abraham.

It was at such a moment that the two archangels appeared. It was a great chance of grace for Lot. Being now poor in heart, Lot could not let go of that chance knowing who they were. Although he did not know exactly why they came to Sodom, he believed it was his chance to recover the grace that he had lost. This kind of attitude opened a way for his salvation.

Lot bowed down with his face to the ground and asked the two archangels to spend the night at his house. The two archangels said they would spend the night in the square, but Lot repeatedly and strongly urged them to come to his house, and they entered his house. Lot prepared food and served them. This act also became a chance for his salvation.

Of course, Lot's salvation from the punishments on Sodom and Gomorrah was God's grace given to him considering Abraham. However, the way of salvation could open for him without violating the justice because he also served the angels of God with all his best and sought the grace of God.

Abraham was one of the main reasons that could save Lot, but salvation is still decided by each one's faith. Therefore, Lot had to show the kind of faith to lead him inside the boundary of salvation. Fortunately, he had enough faith to invite the two archangels to his house and serve them, and he showed that faith with action. This was how he could seize this opportunity of grace.

2. The corrupt Sodomites and the two archangels

"Before they lay down, the men of the city, the men of Sodom, surrounded the house, both young and old, all the people from every quarter; and they called to Lot and said to him, 'Where are the men who came to you tonight? Bring them out to us that we may have relations with them.' But Lot went out to them at the doorway, and shut the door behind him, and said, 'Please, my brothers, do not act wickedly. Now behold, I have two daughters who have not had relations with man; please let me bring them out to you, and do to them whatever you like; only do nothing to these men, inasmuch as they have come under the shelter of my roof.' But they said, 'Stand aside.' Furthermore, they said, 'This one came in as an alien, and already he is acting like a judge; now we will treat you worse than them.' So they pressed hard against Lot and came near to break the door. But the men reached out their hands and brought Lot into the house with them, and shut the door. They struck the men who were at the doorway of the house with blindness, both small and great, so that they wearied themselves trying to find the doorway" **(19:4-11).**

While Lot was serving the two archangels, an incident took place which revealed how corrupt Sodom was.

It was just before they lay down after dinner. Suddenly the people surrounded Lot's house and demanded the two people. Even though they were in the form of human beings, they were distinctively more beautiful than ordinary people.

Sodom was sexually very corrupt (Jude 1:7). And as they saw such beautiful individuals that they had never seen before, they were excited. They were blinded by their lust. They even threatened Lot to give them the two individuals.

Lot went out to them to talk them out of it. In fact, it was an act of risking his life to stand before such agitated people. The situation, however, was not resolved. They wouldn't just back away. Lot begged them not to do anything to his guests saying he would give them his virgin daughters. He wanted to protect the archangels even if it meant he had to sacrifice his own daughters.

Some might wonder how Lot could make such a proposal and if he had the right to do what he wanted with his daughters, even though they were his children. But it was not because Lot did not care about his daughters but he felt he really had to protect those individuals who were of God.

Lot's daughters also understood the situation and they were ready to listen to their father. Lot tried to protect his guests at all costs. Because it was an act out of good intentions, he and his daughters were protected after all. God caused all things to work together for good.

What if Lot was not sitting in the gate when the two archangels arrived at the city? Or, even if he was sitting there, what if he did not invite them into his house or surrendered them to the people at night? If any of these happened, it'd have been difficult for him to be saved.

But Lot was at a place where he could seize the opportunity of grace, and, when it came to him, he did not let go of it. Also, he kept his faith and trust in God even in a situation where his life was threatened and his daughters could have been sacrificed.

Even after hearing the proposal of Lot, the people of Sodom were relentless. Hearing Lot's words that pointed out their wrongdoing, they became furious, and now they wanted to harm him.

Furthermore, they were now trying to put all the blame on Lot. They were saying they had to act the way they were acting only because he tried to become the judge over them. Of course it was not true. They were in fact venting their frustration that was caused because their demands were not granted.

The people in Sodom were not only sexually corrupt. They did not have any sense of morality or ethics. Lot chose the land of Sodom but he couldn't assimilate into the community. In the view of the Sodomites, he was always an alien for he would never join them in their lustful lifestyle.

So, because Lot was not really close to them, they even wanted to harm him as things got heated between them. Of course, their ultimate goal was to have relations with the two individuals in his house. But as Lot stood in their way, they had no reservations about harming him.

As the situation became very serious the two archangels showed their supernatural power that they had kept hidden. They pulled Lot into the house and closed the doors, and blinded the eyes of the people. The two archangels acted according to the physical law in order to check the corruption of the Sodomites in person. But as they had already seen their vicious immorality, they did not have to either hide their identity or keep on following physical laws. The group of which their eyes were blinded was wearied searching for the door.

Blinding their eyes doesn't mean they became completely blind. If they were actually blind for the moment, they wouldn't have tried to find the doors. *"They wearied themselves trying to find the doorway"* means it seemed that they were seeing the door but they couldn't actually locate it.

How could such a thing take place? It was made possible because the two archangels separated the space in which Lot's family was from the one in which the Sodomites were. Even though there are countless angels in the same space, we can't see them unless our spiritual eyes are open. Of course, spiritual space and physical space are different from each other. So, even though angels are very close to us when seen with spiritual eyes, we can't see them unless our spiritual eyes are open.

It is something similar when the two archangels blinded the eyes of the people. Just like we can't see angels with our spiritual eyes closed, the people in Sodom couldn't find the doorway either. It felt like they were in the same space, but they were in two completely different spaces because the two archangels separated them.

Let me give you another allegory. Suppose you expose a dog or a cat to a TV for the first time. Probably they'd think the events on TV as ones happening in their own space. If there is food on the TV screen, they'd probably approach it and try to get it.

In the same way, the people in Sodom, not realizing the spaces were separate, just kept on trying to find the door to go into the house. But of course, they couldn't find the door and they got tired trying. After Lot and his family were saved from this dire situation, they finally escaped from the city of Sodom with the help of the two archangels.

3. The two archangels bring Lot and his family out

"Then the two men said to Lot, 'Whom else have you here? A son-in-law, and your sons, and your daughters, and whomever you have in the city, bring them out of the place; for we are about to destroy this place, because their outcry has become so great before the LORD that the LORD has sent us to destroy it.' Lot went out and spoke to his sons-in-law, who were to marry his daughters, and said, 'Up, get out of this place, for the LORD will destroy the city.' But he appeared to his sons-in-law to be jesting. When morning dawned, the angels urged Lot, saying, 'Up, take your wife and your two daughters who are here, or you will be swept away in the punishment of the city.' But he hesitated. So the men seized his hand and the hand of his wife and the hands of his two daughters, for the compassion of the LORD was upon him; and they brought him out, and put him outside the city" (19:12-16).

Before the escape from Sodom, the two archangels asked Lot who else he had there. Of course, it wasn't because they did not know. The reason why they still asked allows us to feel how much compassion God had for Lot and those who were with him, and that He had given them much grace in consideration of Abraham.

The two archangels came to save him, but in Lot's viewpoint, he felt it was too much to ask the two archangels to save those people who belonged with him, too. Just before the punishment came upon Sodom, he was already embarrassed before God for the fact that he had chosen to live in that land, so he didn't dare ask God anything in that situation.

And yet, God said through the two archangels, *"A son-in-law, and your sons, and your daughters, and whomever you have in the city, bring them out of the place."* God broadened the boundary of salvation for them. God saved Lot considering Abraham, and He gave the chance of salvation even for those who belonged with Lot.

Even if Lot himself was saved, how deeply regretful and how heart-broken would he have been if his family was destroyed without having a chance to repent? Knowing all this, God showed His mercy not just to Lot but also to those who were with him.

God had no desire to destroy anyone. He just eagerly wants to save even just one more soul and lead them to the heavenly kingdom. So, He broadened the boundary of salvation within the limit of not violating justice. Based on this fact, we can understand what a great blessing it is just to accompany somebody who is loved by God.

When the two archangels warned him of the imminent punishment and told him to leave the city of Sodom, what kinds of emotions do you think he had? Leaving the city meant giving up his livelihood. He had to let go of any wealth, fame, or power he had there. If his family wouldn't follow him, he would have to give up his family too.

Moreover, there was no sign of the imminent punishment. He might have thought he would have time to save some of the wealth he had. However, he was told to leave everything behind and get out of the city immediately. Lot believed the words of the archangels and followed the way of salvation. He also explained to his family the way of salvation, as well.

His two daughters and wife listened to him, but the two men engaged to his daughters considered it a joke. They were given a chance of salvation but forsook it. Since they were stained by sins and evil they had no intention at all to give up the life they had in Sodom. God stretched out His loving hands and gave them a chance for salvation, but they wouldn't seize the opportunity because their hearts were full of love for the world (1 John 2:15). On the contrary, Lot did not second-guess what he was told nor did he have any lingering attachments to Sodom. He just obeyed immediately.

On the one hand God showed mercy to Lot considering Abraham, and on the other hand, Lot also showed his faith in obedience and in deeds, so that he could receive the grace of salvation.

But Lot hesitated for a moment despite the urging of the

two archangels that had begun at dawn. It wasn't because Lot had lingering attachment to Sodom. It tells us Lot tried until the end to save as many as possible among those who belonged with him. Just like Noah proclaimed the punishment until the moment he had to close the door of the ark, Lot also tried to let the people know that the punishment was imminent.

Lot had settled in Sodom and had significant wealth, too. He had many people with him other than the two men engaged to his daughters. He wanted to give them the chance for salvation, too. But they were not yet ready to give up their life-styles in Sodom, and they wouldn't go with Lot. Only after he waited until he couldn't wait any longer did he bring his wife and two daughters out of the city in haste. So, it was only his wife and two daughters who had listened to him and escaped.

Even though the punishment and the judgment are proclaimed, salvation can be given only to those who obey in their freewill.

4. God saves Lot in consideration of Abraham

"When they had brought them outside, one said, 'Escape for your life! Do not look behind you, and do not stay anywhere in the valley; escape to the mountains, or you will be swept away.' But Lot said to them, 'Oh no, my lords! Now behold, your servant

> has found favor in your sight, and you have magnified your lovingkindness, which you have shown me by saving my life; but I cannot escape to the mountains, for the disaster will overtake me and I will die; now behold, this town is near enough to flee to, and it is small. Please, let me escape there (is it not small?) that my life may be saved.' He said to him, 'Behold, I grant you this request also, not to overthrow the town of which you have spoken. Hurry, escape there, for I cannot do anything until you arrive there.' Therefore the name of the town was called Zoar" **(19:17-22).**

As things were very pressing, the archangels brought Lot's family outside. Bringing Lot's family outside signifies that the archangels showed the power of riding spiritual space for a moment.

Also, what does it mean by *"Do not look behind you, and do not stay anywhere in the valley; escape to the mountains"?* It spiritually means we have to completely cut off and cast away all the worldly things and fleshly things in us.

Sodom spiritually signifies this corrupt world. Even if we are outside of Sodom, if we still look behind or stay anywhere in the valley, it means we are still attached to the world. In this regard, 'escape to the mountains' means we have to start a new life that is separated from this world.

Lot had made a wrong choice and lived in the corrupt city of Sodom. But he threw away all the worldly things in obedience to the Word of God. He came forward to a new life, and salvation was granted. It is not just that Lot's body came out from the world. According to the command not to look back or stay, he cut off all his attachments to the world in his heart.

As the signs of the disaster were clear, the archangels ordered Lot to escape to the mountains, but he was too afraid to do so. So, he asked for permission to escape to Zoar, which was near Sodom.

It wasn't because Lot still had lingering attachments to Sodom or he wanted to disobey the words of the two archangels. It was just that the signs of the punishment were so fearful. Just by seeing this response of Lot, we can imagine how severe and fearful the punishment of fire was on Sodom and Gomorrah.

But the people in Sodom and Gomorrah were not able to realize the seriousness of the situation. Here, it'd have been better if Lot had escaped to the mountains, having faith in and relying on God. But He did not have such faith.

God still heard Lot's request and showed him His compassion; He allowed him to go to Zoar. Through this event, God caused all things work together for good in the end.

Sodom and Gomorrah at that time were located side by side by a small stream separating them. They were quite populated and big cities. The people from Sodom and Gomorrah moved about freely, and they shared most of the customs and pleasure-seeking cultures. It means corruption in Sodom reflected that of Gomorrah, too.

Zoar was not far from Sodom and Gomorrah, and it was also stained with corrupted culture though not as much as Sodom and Gomorrah. Therefore, Zoar could also be punished together with the other cities. But it was saved because Lot chose that city as his shelter.

It says, *"Behold, I grant you this request also, not to overthrow the town of which you have spoken."* It tells us that Zoar was supposed to be punished but it was spared because of Lot's request. So, the people of Zoar received one more chance.

The residents of Zoar who escaped the punishment clearly witnessed the disaster inflicted upon Sodom and Gomorrah. Cities that were much bigger and more brilliant than their own disappeared into thin air overnight without leaving any trace behind. Also, they heard from Lot's family about why Sodom and Gomorrah were punished and who it was that brought down the punishment. They clearly saw what the consequences of sinful life were.

5. The judgment of fire on Sodom and Gomorrah

"The sun had risen over the earth when Lot came to Zoar. Then

the LORD rained on Sodom and Gomorrah brimstone and fire from the LORD out of heaven, and He overthrew those cities, and all the valley, and all the inhabitants of the cities, and what grew on the ground. But his wife, from behind him, looked back, and she became a pillar of salt. Now Abraham arose early in the morning and went to the place where he had stood before the LORD; and he looked down toward Sodom and Gomorrah, and toward all the land of the valley, and he saw, and behold, the smoke of the land ascended like the smoke of a furnace. Thus it came about, when God destroyed the cities of the valley, that God remembered Abraham, and sent Lot out of the midst of the overthrow, when He overthrew the cities in which Lot lived" **(19:23-29).**

Brimstone and fire rained upon Sodom and Gomorrah as soon as Lot went into the city of Zoar. The consequence was irreversible; Sodom and Gomorrah were completely razed and uninhabitable. God carried out His punishment strictly so that the people of later times could also see and understand what the results of the punishment were.

And there was another kind of disaster; salt was added to the land that the land literally became dead. When Lot first went to Sodom, it was so fertile that the Bible says it was like *"the garden of the LORD, like the land of Egypt."*

Sodom and Gomorrah are known to be located south of the Dead Sea. Dead Sea is literally a 'dead sea' where no life is found. Today, it is presumed Sodom and Gomorrah sank in the Dead Sea due to the ground sinking, and no trace of those cities can be found. It is that no other civilization could be reformed there ever again.

Even though we leave the world behind for a moment, like Lot's family left Sodom, it doesn't mean salvation is guaranteed.

Lot's family left Sodom but his wife did not heed the warning of the archangels and looked back, and she became a pillar of salt. It clearly shows us the result of the inability to give up lingering attachments to the world. Lot and his two daughters could also have had some desire to look back at the city of Sodom. But they listened to the warning of the archangels and overcame the temptation, and eventually they were saved.

The rain of brimstone and fire on Sodom and Gomorrah was so great that even though Abraham lived a considerable distance away he was also able to take note of it. He woke up early in the morning and went to the place where he had met God when he looked toward Sodom and Gomorrah. This tells us that he knew exactly when punishments would be inflicted upon Sodom and Gomorrah.

Abraham believed in the faithful God who always does what He says, so he knew that there would be punishments at the designated point in time. That is why he looked toward Sodom and Gomorrah thinking about Lot and the people of

Sodom and Gomorrah. What kind of person is Abraham?

He implored God not to destroy Sodom only if there were ten righteous men in it. He had the compassion and mercy of God in him, and he wanted that even just one soul would not perish but be saved.

How could it be that God did not know this heart of Abraham? But everything was supposed to be done exactly according to justice, and thus, Sodom had to face the punishment because not even ten righteous men could be found.

When Abraham was looking down toward Sodom and Gomorrah with tremendous sympathy, the smoke of the land ascended like the smoke of a furnace. Sodom and Gomorrah were burning in the rain of brimstone and fire.

One thing must not go unnoticed in regard to punishment on Sodom and Gomorrah. It is that God's punishment did not only come upon the two cities but also their vicinities. Nearby land also became so completely barren that not so much as a single blade of grass could be found.

This means that personal crime will affect one's surroundings as well as the individual. On the contrary, just like Lot was saved thanks to Abraham, if you are with a person who is recognized by God as righteous, you will receive the blessing together with that person.

6. Fathers of Moab and Ammon

"Lot went up from Zoar, and stayed in the mountains, and his two daughters with him; for he was afraid to stay in Zoar; and he stayed in a cave, he and his two daughters. Then the firstborn said to the younger, 'Our father is old, and there is not a man on earth to come in to us after the manner of the earth. Come, let us make our father drink wine, and let us lie with him that we may preserve our family through our father.' So they made their father drink wine that night, and the firstborn went in and lay with her father; and he did not know when she lay down or when she arose. On the following day, the firstborn said to the younger, 'Behold, I lay last night with my father; let us make him drink wine tonight also; then you go in and lie with him, that we may preserve our family through our father.' So they made their father drink wine that night also, and the younger arose and lay with him; and he did not know when she lay down or when she arose. Thus both the daughters of Lot were with child by their father. The firstborn bore a son, and called his name Moab; he is the father of the Moabites to this day. As for the younger, she also bore a son, and called his name Ben-ammi; he is the father of the sons of Ammon to this day" **(19:30-38)**.

Lot went into Zoar, looking for an escape from the punishment, but he was afraid to stay there. From this we can infer the situations of Zoar at that time. The people in Zoar did not turn from their wicked and corrupt lives even after witnessing the punishment on Sodom and Gomorrah.

Lot couldn't help but become afraid because he knew very well why Sodom was punished. He knew that he couldn't stay in Zoar. Witnessing the punishment on Sodom, Lot decided to depart from sins completely, and he had no intention to stay in Zoar a moment longer.

He came out from Zoar with his two daughters and went to the mountain that the archangels mentioned. 'Mountains' symbolizes a spiritually separated place from this world. Lot going up 'to the mountain and staying in a cave' doesn't mean he lived in seclusion. He had commercial exchanges and interchanges with others in nearby cities for a living.

And yet, Lot did not have any interest in the secular world, and his two daughters also followed him. Now, this caused a problem; they couldn't find husbands. They couldn't even think about getting their husbands from those who were in the rebellious world.

Now, something unexpected takes place to the two daughters and Lot who were living in the mountains. The two daughters made their father drunk and lay with him without his knowledge to get offspring. They wanted to keep their family through their father.

It was good that Lot's daughters made up their mind to

begin a new life and didn't try to get their husbands from the people of the world. But since they were looking for the measures within their limited thoughts, they came to use their fleshly thoughts. Eventually, the children they got from their father became the fathers of Moabites and Ammonites.

The result of Lot's two daughters using their fleshly thoughts had an effect throughout generations. Moabites and Ammonites were used as the rod of men for the sons of Israel, when they departed from God's will. But when Israel lived in the will of God, these peoples were under Israel's influence and had to pay tribute to Israel.

So, in the history of human cultivation, Moabites and Ammonites were used as a peripheral element. But how could Lot and his two daughters ever imagine their children and Abraham's children would stand against each other in the future? Using fleshly thoughts led to such a heart-breaking outcome.

What if Lot's two daughters honestly talked about their problems with their father before they did things at their own discretion?

Lot would have probably remembered his uncle Abraham. They couldn't get any husbands in the vicinity, but there must have been people around Abraham who were taught by

Abraham and who tried to live in the truth, without being stained by the world.

Also, if Lot's daughters prayed before God for guidance, they would have gotten this positive idea even if they hadn't consulted with their father. But they only had limited thoughts of their own and acted upon such fleshly thoughts.

However, one thing is clear. Lot and his daughters tried to live a life that was separate from the secular world, even though it meant they had to leave Zoar to the mountain and live a life that would be accompanied with hardship and inconvenience.

This is what is required of the Christians today also. True Christians would have to live a distinguished life apart from the world. They must not follow the lust of the world but try to cut off the world. They have to pray to live by the Word of God and be filled with the Holy Spirit.

In Addition 5

The Four Living Creatures Executed the Judgment of Fire on Sodom and Gomorrah

The punishment on Sodom and Gomorrah serve as an example to people of later generations showing the result of sin. Sodom and Gomorrah became the symbols of sins and were mentioned many times even in the New Testament.

Because it had great significance in history, God did not just send some angels but sent God the Holy Spirit and the two archangels before the actual punishment was inflicted. It was so that the punishment would be carried out in precise justice by checking the situations of Sodom and Gomorrah in person. Because the punishment would also have an effect on the later generations, God the Holy Spirit came there in person accompanied by the two archangels.

As the final verdict was given in justice, the punishments were executed by the 'four living creatures'. As the name suggests, it is a cherub comprised of four living creatures. Each living creature has a head, and on four sides of the head are the faces of a man, a lion, a bull, and an eagle. In total there are four living things that have the four faces. And thus it is called the 'four living creatures'.

The four living creatures are like royal bodyguards that guard God at the closest proximity. They even have the authority to carry out punishments by the command of God. Ezekiel 1:24-26 shows us the appearance and greatness of the authority and dignity of the four living creatures.

It says, *"I also heard the sound of their wings like the sound of abundant waters as they went, like the voice of the Almighty, a sound of tumult like the sound of an army camp; whenever they stood still, they dropped their wings. And there came a voice from above the expanse that was over their heads; whenever they stood still, they dropped their wings. Now above the expanse that was over their heads there was something resembling a throne, like lapis lazuli in appearance; and on that which resembled a throne, high up, was a figure with the appearance of a man."*

Ezekiel 1:14 says, *"And the living beings ran to and fro like bolts of lightning."* If an order of God is given, the four living creatures move like bolts of lightning.

Now, what are the duties of the four living creatures?

They move by the command of God when there are sins that are directly related with God, such as blasphemy, speaking against, or standing against the Holy Spirit. Also, the four living creatures can execute punishments when a whole race or a nation must be punished for their grave sins. Such was a case with Sodom and Gomorrah.

But the roles of each of the four living creatures are different from each other. They are separate, but they always move like one being. And yet, according to the situation, a particular creature will take the leading role. When the punishment of fire was inflicted on Sodom and Gomorrah, the lion creature played the leading role, because it has the authority to give out fire from its mouth.

Because this lion creature has the authority to bring about disasters, it does not open its mouth easily. It opens its mouth only when a punishment is inflicted or when a punishment is to be stopped. The man creature has the authority to command and mobilize cherubim; the eagle creature has the authority to open and close the gates of heaven; and the bull creature has the authority to control the weather conditions.

In the case of the punishment inflicted upon Sodom and Gomorrah, the lion creature played the leading role of bringing down the fire while the eagle creature played an assisting role by opening and closing the gate of heaven.

Abraham

Chapter 9

God Reveals Abraham in His Providence

Abimelech takes Abraham's wife Sarah
"Restore the man's wife, for he is a prophet"
Abimelech king of Gerar's apology and compensation
Abimelech receives an answer by Abraham's prayer

1. Abimelech takes Abraham's wife Sarah

"Now Abraham journeyed from there toward the land of the Negev, and settled between Kadesh and Shur; then he sojourned in Gerar. Abraham said of Sarah his wife, 'She is my sister.' So Abimelech king of Gerar sent and took Sarah. But God came to Abimelech in a dream of the night, and said to him, 'Behold, you are a dead man because of the woman whom you have taken, for she is married'" **(20:1-3).**

The following is an account of when Abraham was staying in Gerar. Abimelech king of Gerar took Sarah to have her as his wife. It was because Abraham had said that Sarah was his sister. It appears to be similar to the incident when Sarah was taken by Pharaoh and then returned. But the spiritual meanings in the two events are different.

In Genesis chapter 12, Abram went down to Egypt to escape

famine. He was afraid that people might kill him to take his wife, so he said Sarah was his sister. Of course, this was not a lie.

In fact she was his half-sister, so it was the best solution he could come up with. But what was the result? Sarah was taken by the Pharaoh anyway. It was a result of using his own fleshly thoughts rather than relying on God completely. Only after he realized his idea was wrong did he receive back his wife by the intervention of God. Abram realized his shortcoming through this event and completely humbled himself.

On the contrary when Sarah was taken by Abimelech king of Gerar, it was not the result of Abraham's fleshly thoughts. It was allowed by God to reveal Abraham.

The faith he had now was completely different from that of the past when Sarah was taken by the Pharaoh. Going through trials for a long time, Abraham's fleshly thoughts were completely demolished, and he now trusted in and relied on God fully and completely.

And his wife being taken by Abimelech, king of Gerar, was done in God's providence. It was one of the steps to allow his descendants to later form a great nation.

Through this occasion, God let the people know clearly what kind of person Abraham was and what kind of authority he had. Furthermore, because it was done in the plan of God, He caused all things to work together for good. The outcome was a blessing for Abraham. God appeared in Abimelech's dream and sternly warned him, saying, *"Behold, you are a dead man because of the woman whom you have taken, for she is married."*

2. "Restore the man's wife, for he is a prophet"

"Now Abimelech had not come near her; and he said, 'LORD, will You slay a nation, even though blameless? Did he not himself say to me, "She is my sister"? And she herself said, "He is my brother." In the integrity of my heart and the innocence of my hands I have done this.' Then God said to him in the dream, 'Yes, I know that in the integrity of your heart you have done this, and I also kept you from sinning against Me; therefore I did not let you touch her. Now therefore, restore the man's wife, for he is a prophet, and he will pray for you and you will live. But if you do not restore her, know that you shall surely die, you and all who are yours.' So Abimelech arose early in the morning and called all his servants and told all these things in their hearing; and the men were greatly frightened. Then Abimelech called Abraham and said to him, 'What have you done to us? And how have I sinned against you, that you have brought on me and on my kingdom a great sin? You have done to me things that ought not to be done.' And Abimelech said to Abraham, 'What have you encountered, that you have done this thing?'" (20:4-10).

But Abimelech said he was innocent because he had not come near her and he had taken her without knowing she was Abraham's wife. Because God knew his innocence, He said in Abimelech's dream, *"Yes, I know that in the integrity of your heart you have done this, and I also kept you from sinning against Me."*

God also told Abimelech how to solve the problem. He said, *"Now therefore, restore the man's wife, for he is a prophet, and he will pray for you and you will live. But if you do not restore her, know that you shall surely die, you and all who are yours."*

I already mentioned that the purpose of God's allowing this happening was to reveal what kind of person Abraham was to the people around him. Thus, God let Abimelech know that Abraham was a prophet and he would live if Abraham prayed for him.

Abimelech couldn't help but become frightened after having this dream. Early the next morning he called all his servants and told them what God had said in his dream. The servants also became frightened. It means Abimelech's servants and men believed the dream he had, and it also tells us they also had good conscience. Had they been evil, they would have reacted in evil ways but they didn't.

Now, Abimelech king of Gerar believed the word of God he heard in his dream and sought the way to resolve that situation.

He called Abraham and asked why Abraham hid the truth

from him. He said, *"What have you done to us? And how have I sinned against you, that you have brought on me and on my kingdom a great sin? You have done to me things that ought not to be done."*

3. Abimelech king of Gerar's apology and compensation

"Abraham said, 'Because I thought, surely there is no fear of God in this place, and they will kill me because of my wife. Besides, she actually is my sister, the daughter of my father, but not the daughter of my mother, and she became my wife; and it came about, when God caused me to wander from my father's house, that I said to her, "This is the kindness which you will show to me: everywhere we go, say of me, 'He is my brother.'"' Abimelech then took sheep and oxen and male and female servants, and gave them to Abraham, and restored his wife Sarah to him. Abimelech said, 'Behold, my land is before you; settle wherever you please.' To Sarah he said, 'Behold, I have given your brother a thousand pieces of silver; behold, it is your vindication before all who are with you, and before all men you are cleared'" **(Genesis 20:11-16).**

When asked by Abimelech king of Gerar, Abraham said he was afraid that people there might kill him to take his wife, because there was no fear of God in that place. He also added that Sarah was actually his sister, too.

Terah, the father of Abraham, remarried and gave birth to Sarah after Abraham's mother died, so she was Abraham's half-sister.

Hearing this, although Abimelech had taken Sarah thinking Sarah was only Abraham's sister, he still wanted to compensate Abraham and Sarah for their mental distress. It shows Abimelech had a relatively good conscience.

If Abimelech had been evil, would he have tried to compensate Abraham? He could have said he didn't have to make up for anything because it was Abraham who had lied to him. But Abimelech didn't.

He didn't just return Sarah to Abraham but as a token of his apology he gave him land on which Abraham could dwell, and he gave him sheep and oxen and male and female servants.

Furthermore, he said to Sarah, *"Behold, I have given your brother a thousand pieces of silver; behold, it is your vindication before all who are with you, and before all men you are cleared."* He tried to resolve all the unpleasant situations in goodness.

4. Abimelech receives an answer by Abraham's prayer

"Abraham prayed to God, and God healed Abimelech and his

wife and his maids, so that they bore children. For the LORD had closed fast all the wombs of the household of Abimelech because of Sarah, Abraham's wife" (Genesis 20:17-18).

Since Abimelech acted in goodness, God gave him grace through Abraham. When Abimelech took Sarah, God closed fast all the wombs of the household of Abimelech. But when Abraham prayed, God healed Abimelech and his wife and his maid servants so they could bear children.

God manifested such a miracle to Abimelech and his household to let the people see what kind of person Abraham was.

As for Abimelech, who was the king, what could have been the greatest interest? He didn't lack wealth, fame, or power. His biggest concern was his heir. For this reason God let Abraham pray for this matter and resolved his situation. Through this event, God let the people keep the existence and identity of Abraham in their minds.

God who knows about all situations let the people be impressed about Abraham in the most certain way, as to what kind of power he had. Along with that, He blessed them greatly, too. It shows this incident where Sarah was taken was not caused by Abraham's fleshly thoughts, but it was in the providence of God. It might have seemed that it was a loss for Abraham, but we can see in the end it was blessing for him and God was glorified.

Abraham

Chapter 10

Isaac the Promised Seed and Ishmael

- Isaac was born to Abraham at the age of 100
- Ishmael mocked Isaac
- Hagar and Ishmael sent out into the wilderness
- Ishmael takes an Egyptian wife
- Abraham and Abimelech made a covenant
- Seven ewe lambs as a witness of digging the well

1. Isaac was born to Abraham at the age of 100

"Then the LORD took note of Sarah as He had said, and the LORD did for Sarah as He had promised. So Sarah conceived and bore a son to Abraham in his old age, at the appointed time of which God had spoken to him. Abraham called the name of his son who was born to him, whom Sarah bore to him, Isaac. Then Abraham circumcised his son Isaac when he was eight days old, as God had commanded him. Now Abraham was one hundred years old when his son Isaac was born to him. Sarah said, "God has made laughter for me; everyone who hears will laugh with me." And she said, "Who would have said to Abraham that Sarah would nurse children? Yet I have borne him a son in his old age" (21:1-7).

When God told Abraham He would give him a son through Sarah, she laughed because she couldn't believe it. But God gave the promised son not because of Sarah but because Abraham faithfully believed in the word of God. Isaac, the promised seed, was born precisely at the designated time.

People might think God could have given Isaac to Abraham a little earlier, but everything has its proper timing (Ecclesiastes 3:1). Because He knows everything, it is God who sets the timing. The timing that has been set by God cannot be shortened just because people are in a hurry. Therefore, we should not become impatient with our own thoughts. We have to believe unchangingly in the will and providence of God.

Abraham believed God's promise to give him a son without a shred of doubt. Even with the passage of time, his faith never wavered. Finally, when the time that had been set by God had come, the visible fruit was given. We should not judge God's works at our discretion understanding the fact that God's thoughts are different from the thoughts of men.

Now, what is the reason that God intentionally said 'Abraham in his old age'? It is because it puts an emphasis on the fact that Abraham was physically unable to beget a child, but God worked according to his faith. In this way, faith is to hope and believe in what you cannot expect or imagine in reality.

Abraham named his son Isaac, meaning 'laughter'. This name had been given by God before the son was born (Genesis 17:9). Abraham did not forget what God had told him, and he followed it as spoken by God.

Also, Abraham circumcised Isaac when he was eight days old. He obeyed God's command written in Genesis 17:12, *"And every male among you who is eight days old shall be circumcised throughout your generations, a servant who is born in the house or who is bought with money from any foreigner, who is not of your descendants."*

When God commanded Abraham to conduct circumcision, he circumcised all men in his household on that day without any delay. And as Abraham does not use any thoughts of men but totally obeys God's words, how can he not be lovely in the eyes of God?

God mentions that Abraham was 100 years old when he begot Isaac. It was to say once again that Isaac was born at the most appropriate time in God's providence.

After giving birth to Isaac, Sarah said, *"God has made laughter for me; everyone who hears will laugh with me."* She laughed when she had heard God would give a son. She laughed at that time because she couldn't believe what God had said.

But eventually, Sarah gave birth to a son as God had spoken and she came to laugh once again. This laughter was the laughter of joy. She must have been filled with thanks and joy since she was actually able to experience what she had not been able to believe.

Repenting of her unbelief, she could laugh with joy and thanks to God. Also, her laughter contained shyness, too. She felt somewhat timid to say to people that she gave birth at a very old age.

She also said, *"Who would have said to Abraham that Sarah would nurse children? Yet I have borne him a son in his old age."* It is that she emphasized once again God did something impossible.

With human knowledge, it was absolutely impossible for Sarah to give birth to and nurse a child at her age. And she meant to say such a thing was made possible by God's power.

2. Ishmael mocked Isaac

"The child grew and was weaned, and Abraham made a great feast on the day that Isaac was weaned. Now Sarah saw the son of Hagar the Egyptian, whom she had borne to Abraham, mocking Isaac. Therefore she said to Abraham, 'Drive out this maid and her son, for the son of this maid shall not be an heir with my son Isaac.' The matter distressed Abraham greatly because Ishmael was his son. But God said to Abraham, 'Do not be distressed because of the lad and your maid; whatever Sarah tells you, listen to her, for through Isaac your descendants shall be named. And of the son of the maid I will make a nation also, because he is your

descendant'" (21:8-13).

As for Isaac, who was the promised seed, God guided his whole life from his conception, birth and throughout his growth. He grew up in the kind interventions of God. On the day Isaac was weaned Abraham held a great feast, giving thanks to God for His grace.

But as Isaac grew up, the buried conflict between Hagar and Sarah began to resurface. In the past, when Hagar was with the child of Abraham, Sarah mistreated her. Eventually, Hagar had to run from Sarah. But she came back after she met an angel of God and received the word of promise about her son who was to be born.

Sarah acknowledged that her actions went overboard, and Hagar also obeyed her lady Sarah. On the surface, peace was restored. But they did not get rid of hard-feelings towards each other held in the heart, and thus the peace was only momentary and the peace ended when a situation similar to the past was recreated.

Seeing Ishmael mocking the young Isaac, Sarah asked Abraham to dismiss Hagar and Ishmael. Even though a significant length of time had passed, Sarah still kept the heart of untruth in her, just suppressing it at one corner of her heart. If she had understood Abraham's heart just a little bit, and if she had had just a little bit of his good heart, she wouldn't have requested such a thing.

If Sarah's heart had been broader and better, she'd have cared for Ishmael like her own, because he too was Abraham's son. Also, Ishmael's mocking Isaac wouldn't have looked like real mocking but just a simple prank or playing around between little brothers.

Then, Hagar could have been touched by Sarah's heart of goodness, and they would've been able to maintain the peace. But because Sarah was not capable of showing such an act of goodness, Abraham was once again heart-broken. Ishmael was not the heir who would continue the orthodox family of Abraham, but Abraham was still worried when Sarah asked him to send him away.

I've been explaining that Sarah's heart is not in accordance with the truth, but the same goes for Hagar and Ishmael as well.

Sarah wouldn't have come up with the idea of throwing them out just because of one incident. Hard-feelings had been piling up over a period of time, and eventually, she exploded when she saw Ishmael mocking Isaac. Before Sarah felt threatened allowing Ishmael near Isaac, Hagar and Ishmael had also acted out their roles as well.

Hagar was a maid-servant, so she should have served Sarah as she had done before, but she didn't. Ishmael did not care for Isaac as his own brother either. Eventually peace was broken because neither of them understood the other. Now Hagar and Ishmael had to go away. Seeing all this, Abraham had to suffer the pain in his heart.

Although Ishmael was not the promised seed who would continue the orthodox genealogy, he too was a lovely son like Isaac. Of course, Abraham knew very well that the providence of God would be fulfilled by Isaac, but it didn't mean he did not love Ishmael or that he would discriminate against him.

God knew about these concerns of Abraham and told him to send Hagar and Ishmael away as Sarah demanded. Until God had given him direction, Abraham couldn't keep from worrying about this situation, but when he received God's instructions, he obeyed immediately without any hesitation. One might think it'd be better to gently advise Sarah and make her understand rather than kicking Hagar and Ishmael out.

But Abraham didn't utilize any thoughts of his own. He considered his thoughts, his goodness, or his righteousness as nothing before God's Word. Such obedience comes from a person who completely trusts God. Because his fleshly thoughts had been shattered through trials, he obeyed God's Word in any situation. However, if Ishmael had kept on wandering without destination or his family line had ceased to exist, how could it not have been very painful for Abraham?

So, in consideration of Abraham's heart and his caring for

Ishmael, God promised him that He would form a nation through Ishmael, too..

3. Hagar and Ishmael sent out into the wilderness

"So Abraham rose early in the morning and took bread and a skin of water and gave them to Hagar, putting them on her shoulder, and gave her the boy, and sent her away. And she departed and wandered about in the wilderness of Beersheba. When the water in the skin was used up, she left the boy under one of the bushes. Then she went and sat down opposite him, about a bowshot away, for she said, 'Do not let me see the boy die.' And she sat opposite him, and lifted up her voice and wept. God heard the lad crying; and the angel of God called to Hagar from heaven and said to her, 'What is the matter with you, Hagar? Do not fear, for God has heard the voice of the lad where he is. Arise, lift up the lad, and hold him by the hand, for I will make a great nation of him.' Then God opened her eyes and she saw a well of water; and she went and filled the skin with water and gave the lad a drink" (21:14-19).

As soon as Abraham had received the word from God, he rose early in the morning and sent Hagar and Ishmael away. He didn't think, "I'll send them out in several days." He obeyed

God's word as soon as he received it. He didn't give them any money or try to comfort them with fleshly affection. He didn't even give them any servants for protection.

He just gave them bread and a skin of water. Abraham was a very wealthy man, and it might look heartless. Through his act, however, we can see once again how well and absolutely Abraham obeyed God's word.

In fact Abraham's act stemmed from spiritual love. In a physical sense of course he'd want to give them money and servants. But Abraham gave them the greatest fortune that couldn't be compared with anything in the world. It was reverence and reliance on God the Creator.

Instead of giving them some of his wealth or servants, he let them have the willingness to rely on God alone who is the source of all blessings and the governor of life and death. Wealth could be squandered and people can also leave any time. But if we keep on trusting and relying on God, He will never turn His face away from us.

Because Abraham knew this fact very well, he wanted Hagar and Ishmael to revere God in any situation. That is why he didn't give them anything physical they could depend on. Because Abraham was a man of faith and spiritual love, he wanted Hagar and Ishmael to experience the living God firsthand and to dwell in Him.

There was also another reason why Abraham gave them only bread and a skin of water. Of course he committed everything into God's hands, and yet he didn't want them to go very far away. He wished that they could settle in a place where he could hear about them. It was the father's heart desiring that his son would live nearby.

Through this love and obedience of Abraham, Hagar and Ishmael experienced a work of God and His delicate touch guiding them. They left only with bread and a skin of water, and soon they ran out of food and water. Hagar was wandering in the wilderness of Beersheba. She sat with her son and wept thinking they were going to die.

At the moment the angel of God appeared and comforted her, and gave her the promise that Ishmael would form a great people. And, as God opened her eyes, she saw a well of water; and she went and filled the skin with water and let the boy drink it.

It was not that God created a well in an instant for Hagar and Ishmael. It was actually there but she just couldn't see it. God helped her see it by opening her eyes. God had prepared it knowing when Hagar and Ishmael would come to that place.

Hagar and Ishmael could receive this help of God only through Abraham. Hagar couldn't expect the helping hand of God because she lacked the faith. She just wept thinking her son would die. But God helped Hagar and Ishmael seeing the faith of Abraham who committed everything into His hands.

4. Ishmael takes an Egyptian wife

"God was with the lad, and he grew; and he lived in the wilderness and became an archer. He lived in the wilderness of Paran, and his mother took a wife for him from the land of Egypt" (21:20-21).

God protected Ishmael until he grew up. He kept His promise concerning Ishmael. We can see blessings came upon those who were with Abraham, the man of faith.

But Hagar and Ishmael didn't understand where the blessings came from. Ishmael was protected by God and raised in God's care to form a nation. All this was possible because Abraham left everything to God with faith.

Abraham earnestly hoped Hagar and Ishmael would revere God in their lives by experiencing Him. However, even though they were saved from the threshold of death, they considered it lightly. They didn't understand the grace and blessing of God deep in their hearts.

We can infer this from the fact that Hagar took an Egyptian woman as Ishmael's wife. Hagar was an Egyptian but Ishmael was Abraham's son. She also knew that Abraham served God and he'd like his son to serve God as well. Ishmael was circumcised along with Abraham by the command of God.

However, Hagar let her son take a Gentile woman for his wife. This is the proof that she did not really believe in God even though she had experienced the hands of God when she was about to die in the wilderness of Beersheba, running away from Sarah.

If she had really believed in God, she'd have let him take a wife from one of Abraham's people who believed and revered God. Abraham must have taught her so much, but she didn't listen. As a result of this, there was another Gentile nation formed that stood against Israel.

Also, as a result of Ishmael marrying a Gentile woman, he lost what little reverence he had for God and quickly departed from God. This tells us that no matter how many times we experience the power of God and witness His wonderful works, unless we make them a part of our own faith, they are of no use.

Hagar and Ishmael had witnessed that God was with Abraham and learned how Abraham served God when they were living with him. Also, they must have heard many things about who God is and how they were supposed to serve Him. They also experienced the power of God firsthand. And yet, they didn't really believe in God in their hearts and thus they began to drift away from God.

5. Abraham and Abimelech made a covenant

"Now it came about at that time that Abimelech and Phicol, the commander of his army, spoke to Abraham, saying, 'God is with you in all that you do; now therefore, swear to me here by God that you will not deal falsely with me or with my offspring or with my posterity, but according to the kindness that I have shown to you, you shall show to me and to the land in which you have sojourned.' Abraham said, 'I swear it.' But Abraham complained to Abimelech because of the well of water which the servants of Abimelech had seized. And Abimelech said, 'I do not know who has done this thing; you did not tell me, nor did I hear of it until today.'' Abraham took sheep and oxen and gave them to Abimelech, and the two of them made a covenant" **(Genesis 21:22-27).**

There was an event in which God let the people in the land clearly understand the identity of Abraham. It is the incident where Abraham's wife, Sarah, was taken by Abimelech, king of Gerar. After this occasion Abraham was known to the people as a prophet who was loved and attested to by God and with whom they didn't dare interfere.

That is why a king, Abimelech and the commander of his army came to Abraham and said, *"God is with you in all that you do."* Because Abraham was known to all peoples around the land, he could set up a base of his livelihood among many other races and lay the foundation of Israel's formation.

If the people there had considered Abraham merely as one of the chiefs, they must have tried to make him submit to them every chance they had. But he was considered as a prophet of God with whom they could not interfere, and he was free of any kind of threat.

Of course, Abraham had the power to protect himself and those who belonged to him, but other races didn't even consider harming him because he had the evidence of God being with him. Furthermore, Abimelech king of Gerar was asking Abraham not to harm him and his posterity. It tells us about Abraham's strength and clarity of the evidence of God being with him at that time.

Abimelech knew how strong Abraham was, and he could imagine how strong Abraham's descendants would be. That is why he asked Abraham not to deal falsely even with his posterity. Abraham agreed, and pointed out to Abimelech that Abimelech's men took his wells by force.

Wells around Palestine at that time were very important assets. Losing wells was a very serious problem directly related with the survival of the nomads. After Abraham pointed out this fact, Abimelech said he was not aware of it. He was indirectly asking for forgiveness for it had happened without his knowledge.

From this we can infer that Abimelech didn't have any

intention to lie to Abraham or cause any trouble. It was because Abimelech not only acknowledged that God was with Abraham, but that Abraham was powerful as well. As Abimelech admitted his mistake, Abraham did not try to suppress him with his power but made a gesture of peace by giving Abimelech sheep and oxen to make a covenant.

6. Seven ewe lambs as a witness of digging the well

"Then Abraham set seven ewe lambs of the flock by themselves. Abimelech said to Abraham, 'What do these seven ewe lambs mean, which you have set by themselves?' He said, 'You shall take these seven ewe lambs from my hand so that it may be a witness to me, that I dug this well.' Therefore he called that place Beersheba, because there the two of them took an oath. So they made a covenant at Beersheba; and Abimelech and Phicol, the commander of his army, arose and returned to the land of the Philistines. Abraham planted a tamarisk tree at Beersheba, and there he called on the name of the LORD, the Everlasting God. And Abraham sojourned in the land of the Philistines for many days" **(Genesis 21:28-34).**

Abraham did not ask for compensation but rather gave him seven ewe lambs to reconfirm his ownership of the well. They made a covenant about the well, and called the place Beersheba, which means 'well of the oath'.

Even though the other party clearly did something wrong, Abraham only tried to pursue peace. At the same time, he made an oath with Abimelech in order to prevent any further conflicts. He understood the human mind very well. He always wanted to accept others and have peace.

Here the number seven represents perfection. It signifies Abraham's actions were truthful before God. Abraham made sure the ownership of the well, which is the source of production, was with him, through the seven ewe lambs, which also represents production.

If Abraham only tried to see who was right and who was wrong, Abimelech would have just backed away rather than truly regretting his mistake. This cannot be true peace. If the situations allowed, he could have tried to take the well away again. For this reason, rather than asking for compensation, Abraham gave him the price for the well. Through this incident, Abimelech submitted to Abraham from his heart and never tried to take the well again.

From these proceedings we can understand the wisdom, generosity, and love Abraham had. He was wise in dealing with men, and he also had a broad enough heart to seek other's interests. Also, he did not lift himself up before others with the things he had, but he only humbled himself and wanted to serve others.

Abraham had not only a great power and authority but also humbleness and sense of service. This is the reason why he could have peace with all other races around his household. He accepted the peoples around him with gentleness so that he could keep his possessions and make his foundations firm. (Psalm 37:11).

After Abimelech made the oath and went back to the land of the Philistines, Abraham planted a tamarisk tree at Beersheba as a symbol of this event before God. The oath was made between men, but he wanted it to be recognized by God, too. If we are acknowledged by God like Abraham, then we can be protected and be guided to prosperity in all things.

Abraham first built altars before God wherever he went so he could be guaranteed and guided by God. This is the attitude of someone who completely trusts, relies on, and obeys God. For this reason, as said, *"Abraham sojourned in the land of the Philistines for many days,"* he lived in absolute protection even in the land of the Gentiles.

Abraham's life after Genesis Chapter 20

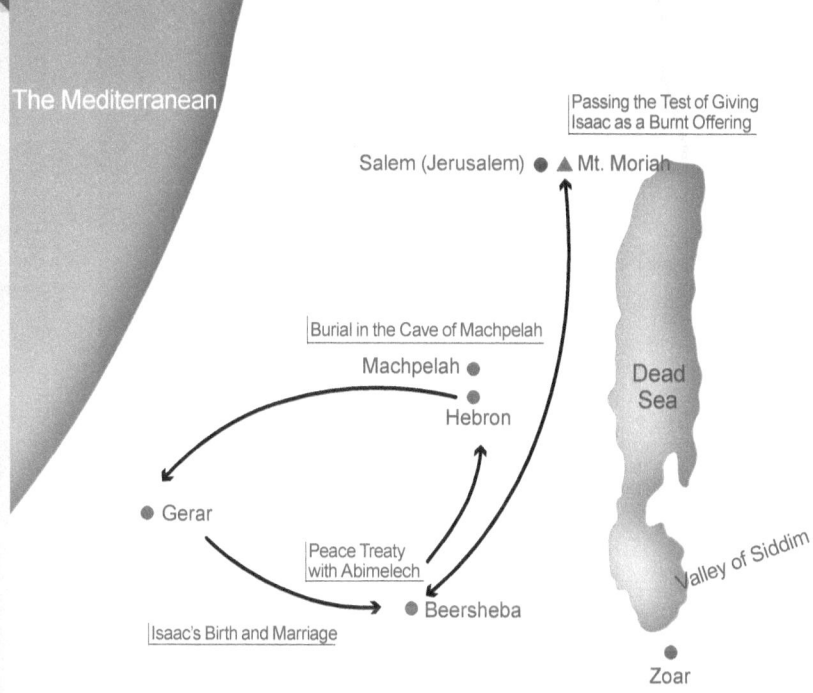

❶ Moving south from Hebron, living at Gerar for a while (Genesis 20)
❷ Begetting Isaac at age 100 (Genesis 21)
❸ Making an oath with Abimelech at Beersheba, planting a tamarisk tree (Genesis 21)
❹ Giving Isaac as a burnt offering at Mt. Moriah (Genesis 22)
❺ Sarah dies and is buried in the cave of Machpelah (Genesis 23)
❻ Getting Isaac's wife from Haran (Genesis 24)
❼ Begetting six sons from Keturah (Genesis 25)
❽ Abraham dies at age 175 and is buried in cave of Machpelah (Genesis 25)

Chapter 11

The Blessings of Jehovah Jireh on Abraham

- Giving Isaac as a burnt offering
- Taking Isaac to Mount Moriah
- Complete obedience of Abraham and Isaac
- "Now I know that you fear God"
- God prepares a ram for the burnt offering
- Established as the Father of Faith
- A wife for Isaac, the promised seed

1. Giving Isaac as a burnt offering

"Now it came about after these things, that God tested Abraham, and said to him, 'Abraham!' And he said, 'Here I am.' He said, 'Take now your son, your only son, whom you love, Isaac, and go to the land of Moriah, and offer him there as a burnt offering on one of the mountains of which I will tell you'" **(22:1-2)**.

By the trials he had gone through, Abraham came to have faith with which he could always say 'Yes' to God. Now God called him and commanded him to offer Isaac as a burnt offering.

A sacrificial animal is cut into pieces separating the flesh from the bones and then it is burnt as a pleasing aroma to God. But God commanded Abraham to cut not an animal but a man, his own son, into pieces and to offer him as a burnt offering.

This was not just to give his only son. For Abraham, offering Isaac as a burnt offering meant something more than offering everything he had. It's because of the spiritual meaning that Isaac carried.

Isaac was the promised seed through which God would give Abraham his descendants. God had promised Abraham his descendants would be as many as the stars in the sky. And Isaac was the son given by God to fulfill this promise.

So, if he gave up Isaac, you'd think the promise of God would have been impossible to be fulfilled. Even the 25 years of waiting and all the efforts in raising Isaac until that day would be in vain.

Even in this situation, Abraham did not use any fleshly thoughts. He did not give any excuses before God. He did not try to reason with God either. God called Abraham and tested him to confirm Abraham's complete obedience and faith. God didn't explain why He was commanding him to offer Isaac or what He would do if he did offer Isaac.

This was the moment when Abraham's love for God and faith in Him could be truly revealed. God did not test him because he had any sin or form of evil. He had already cast off all forms of evil and demolished all his fleshly thoughts, but God needed to prove that he was worthy and perfect to be established as the Father of Faith through this final test.

It was a test given so that God could accept the aroma

of love and faith that was coming out from the depth of Abraham's heart, establish him as the Father of Faith and give him blessings upon blessings.

2. Taking Isaac to Mount Moriah

"So Abraham rose early in the morning and saddled his donkey, and took two of his young men with him and Isaac his son; and he split wood for the burnt offering, and arose and went to the place of which God had told him. On the third day Abraham raised his eyes and saw the place from a distance. Abraham said to his young men, 'Stay here with the donkey, and I and the lad will go over there; and we will worship and return to you.' Abraham took the wood of the burnt offering and laid it on Isaac his son, and he took in his hand the fire and the knife. So the two of them walked on together" **(22:3-6).**

Abraham woke early the next day and together with Isaac they left for the place of which God had told him. Even though God did not tell him all the details, he obeyed immediately and left early in the morning.

He did not have any fleshly thoughts or hesitation. Even though it was something very difficult to understand with human thoughts, he obeyed immediately because he trusted God completely. Because he believed there was the good will of God, he did not have any misunderstanding or resentment either.

But rather he was thankful that God recognized his love and faith even to the extent to give him such a command. He felt the heart of God in giving him the test to offer his only son Isaac as a burnt offering. So, he did not worry but just followed the will of God with joy and thanksgiving.

In the past, Abraham obeyed God's command telling him to *"Go forth from your country, and from your relatives and from your father's house, to the land which I will show you,"* and just left without knowing where to go. This time also, he obeyed immediately when he heard from God, *"go to the land of Moriah, and offer him there as a burnt offering on one of the mountains of which I will tell you."*

Moreover, he prepared all the necessary things for giving the burnt offering. He took two men and even the firewood for the sacrifice. He wouldn't thoughtlessly prepare some wood after he would get to the place. He didn't pretend to be obeying hoping that God would change His command. He sincerely was going to offer his son as a burnt offering and prepared himself accordingly.

But today many pastors preach that Abraham was very reluctant at that time. They say he had agonizing pain during the three days' journey to Moriah. But Abraham did not have any sorrow or agony.

His heart was not heavy during his three-day journey to Moriah. But rather he hurried himself. His face was not filled with any concerns. He was not looking sadly at his son, Isaac. He was full of joy and thanksgiving as he had always been.

How could such actions come out? It's because he had such complete faith in God by which he believed God could even bring someone back from the dead (Hebrews 11:17-19).

Three days after he left home, Abraham raised his eyes and looked at the place that God had pointed out to him. It was not because he hesitated or he had second thoughts before offering Isaac. It was that he reaffirmed his will to fulfill the Word of God completely.

Abraham made his two young men wait there and had Isaac carry the firewood for the burnt offering. He took in his hand the fire and the knife. And He had a reason to leave the two men behind.

What if he took the two men with him? If they saw Abraham trying to cut Isaac and give him as a burnt offering, they would have tried to stop him. It was something they could never understand. They were not at the spiritual level that would allow them to participate in Abraham's march of faith, and thus, Abraham could not bring those two men with him.

Fleshly people use fleshly thoughts, and they cannot understand spiritual things. They only seek fleshly methods within their own thoughts, and this hinders things from being done in spiritual ways. Even though they are told God's will and methods, they just take care of things as they see fit.

For this reason, when he was leaving home to offer Isaac as a burnt offering, he did not say a word to his wife Sarah. He just left early in the morning. If he had told Sarah everything, would she have easily agreed?

Because she still had fleshly thoughts and forms of evil, she would have definitely disagreed and tried to stop Abraham. Knowing this very well, Abraham had to leave without telling Sarah anything.

When he was obeying God's word, Abraham did not waver no matter what the situation or circumstances. He did not change his mind or attitude midway either. God accepted this beautiful aroma of Abraham's heart and caused all things to work together for good.

3. Complete obedience of Abraham and Isaac

"Isaac spoke to Abraham his father and said, 'My father!' And he said, 'Here I am, my son.' And he said, 'Behold, the fire and the

wood, but where is the lamb for the burnt offering?' Abraham said, 'God will provide for Himself the lamb for the burnt offering, my son.' So, the two of them walked on together. Then they came to the place of which God had told him; and Abraham built the altar there and arranged the wood, and bound his son Isaac and laid him on the altar, on top of the wood. Abraham stretched out his hand and took the knife to slay his son" **(22:7-10).**

Isaac thought there was something strange while they were going up the mountain. There were the fire and wood for the burnt offering but no lamb to offer. He wondered about it and asked Abraham.

"God will provide for Himself the lamb for the burnt offering, my son," Abraham replied. Abraham didn't say so to hide the truth from Isaac but it was to commit everything into God's hands.

We see Isaac did not resist at all when Abraham bound him to offer him as a burnt offering. He was willing to obey his father in any situation. Therefore, Abraham did not have to hide what he had to do. But here, saying 'the sacrifice is you' and saying 'God will provide for Himself the lamb for the burnt offering,' have very different levels of goodness.

Even in the same situations, the words we speak will be very different depending on the goodness we have in us. Here, we should not think that Abraham imagined or hoped some other sacrifices were being prepared to replace Isaac. He said what he had said because he knew and believed everything was in God's plan and God was leading him.

After he arrived at the place for the burnt offering, Abraham immediately began the preparations to offer Isaac as a burnt offering. He built an altar, arranged the wood, bound Isaac and laid him on the altar, and took the knife. Was his heart shaken when he actually had to kill his own son, due to his affection for him?

Was he agonizing in sorrow and lamentation? Not at all! Up to the moment he was about to kill Isaac with the knife, he did not use any fleshly thoughts of a man. He just obeyed God's Word without swaying at all. One might say he looks like a heartless father, but it was actually to love God first and the most.

If one has determined to do the will of God, it is the heart of spirit to carry it out without changing of the mind. They wouldn't give such excuses as, "I tried hard but because these things happened I couldn't go through with it," or "When I thought about it again, I thought this way was better and that's what I did."

But if you do something you decided to do out of reluctance, thinking you don't have a choice because it's something that you've already decided to do, then it is not true obedience either. When Abraham was giving Isaac as a burnt offering, he had peace up until the last moment. He did not pretend to have peace only outwardly but he had true peace in him. He never lost joy and thanksgiving.

Isaac did not hear from his father in detail about why his father had to give him as a burnt offering. Abraham just said it was the will of God without giving him any more explanation. And yet, Isaac did not resist or oppose but only followed his father's will quietly.

Even though it meant he was giving his life, he just followed his father, and this shows how much he believed in God and his father Abraham. Isaac knew that his father Abraham always knew God's will very well and obeyed it all the time. That is why he was convinced whatever Abraham was doing was in accordance with God's will.

Had he not had such trust, it would have been very difficult to just keep quiet even though it was his father's will. This clearly tells us how much Isaac trusted Abraham his father. Namely, we can see Abraham had spiritual trust not only with God but also with his son Isaac.

Abraham had numerous communications with God. So, even though God commanded him something he couldn't really understand, he would have obeyed considering all his past experiences and the word of God he had received from God.

But it was different for Isaac. Isaac had never heard God's Word directly. Of course, he had seen, experienced, and heard about the living God and His faithfulness through his father Abraham, but now his own life was at stake.

In such a situation, Isaac just heard from Abraham that it was God's will to give him as a burnt offering. And yet, he didn't doubt his father's word at all. He didn't try to escape or avoid the situation, or reason with his father.

4. "Now I know that you fear God"

"But the angel of the LORD called to him from heaven and said, 'Abraham, Abraham!' And he said, 'Here I am.' He said, 'Do not stretch out your hand against the lad, and do nothing to him; for now I know that you fear God, since you have not withheld your son, your only son, from Me'" (22:11-12).

When Abraham was just about to lay the knife on Isaac, he heard, "Abraham, Abraham." God had already accepted Abrahams' heart and all his actions as beautiful aroma, and He sent His angel to call him.

Abraham replied, "Here I am." It was not like he was waiting for somebody to call him and he replied immediately. He did not have any wish for God to take away the command given to him. Because Abraham was acting without any hesitation, the angel was in more of a hurry. That is why the angel urgently called out twice, "Abraham, Abraham."

As Abraham showed his perfect faith and obedience up until the last moment, God spoke through His angel saying, *"Do not stretch out your hand against the lad, and do nothing to him; for now I know that you fear God, since you have not withheld your son, your only son, from Me."*

God acknowledged Abraham's love, faith, and reverence toward God. Then, does that mean God didn't know that Abraham revered God?

God knows everything and He knew how Abraham would pass the test. He knew the depths of Abraham's heart and his reverence in God. But the reason why God still let him go through this test was so that his future position as the Father of Faith and the future blessings would not be objected to by Satan. It was so that Abraham's faith was certainly revealed even before Satan.

Therefore, when God said, *"for now I know that you fear God,"* it was expression of His joy to gain Abraham, who could be considered one of the best fruits in the history of mankind.

Now, since he had passed the test, could Abraham just go back home with his son Isaac? Of course not! Abraham didn't have to give his son as a burnt offering, but he still had to give a burnt offering because it is what he had decided to give to God.

God did not tell him 'Do not offer a burnt offering'. What God said was merely 'Do not touch Isaac'.

5. God prepares a ram for the burnt offering

> *"Then Abraham raised his eyes and looked, and behold, behind him a ram caught in the thicket by his horns; and Abraham went and took the ram and offered him up for a burnt offering in the place of his son. Abraham called the name of that place The LORD Will Provide, as it is said to this day, 'In the mount of the LORD it will be provided'"* **(22:13-14).**

Abraham needed a substitute sacrifice that would be offered in place of Isaac. God moved his heart and he looked. He found a ram that God had prepared for him. It was caught in the thicket by his horns. He offered it up as a burnt offering in place of his son. Then he named the place 'Jehovah Jireh.'

It means 'The LORD Will Provide' and that God will always look after the needs of the believers.

Next it says, *"In the mount of the LORD it will be provided."* 'In the mount of the LORD' symbolizes the route through which God's plan is fulfilled in His will. Through the test of offering his only son, Isaac, God established Abraham as the 'Father of Faith', and this was also in the plan, providence and will of God.

So, *"In the mount of the LORD it will be provided"* means all things were prepared and fulfilled as God had planned. Now, being moved greatly by God's delicate and gentle guidance, Abraham offered the burnt offering with joy and thanksgiving.

Abraham had no reservation or hesitation when offering Isaac as a burnt offering. Still, there are no words that could express his feelings adequately when he received his son back just before his death. He was even more touched as God had accepted all his heart and actions and had prepared a ram that could be offered in place of his son.

6. Established as the Father of Faith

> *"Then the angel of the LORD called to Abraham a second time from heaven, and said, 'By Myself I have sworn, declares the LORD, because you have done this thing and have not withheld your son, your only son, indeed I will greatly bless you, and I will greatly multiply your seed as the stars of the heavens and as the sand which is on the seashore; and your seed shall possess the gate of their enemies. In your seed all the nations of the earth shall be blessed, because you have obeyed My voice.' So Abraham returned to his young men, and they arose and went together to Beersheba; and Abraham lived at Beersheba"* **(22:15-19).**

As Abraham passed this test, which was to give his only son Isaac as a burnt offering, God gave him a promise of blessing. He said, *"because you have done this thing and have not withheld your son, your only son, indeed I will greatly bless you, and I will greatly multiply your seed as the stars of the heavens and as the sand which is on the seashore; and your seed shall possess the gate of their enemies. In your seed all the nations of the earth shall be blessed, because you have obeyed My voice."*

What is the reason Abraham received such a blessing?

God says the reason was, *"because you have obeyed My voice."* The surest and easiest way to receive blessings and answers to prayers is to obey God's Word.

Abraham could willingly offer the most precious thing to him because he loved God so much. It is very similar to God's love who gave His only begotten Son for mankind. That is why God established him as the Father of Faith and made him the source of blessings..

7. A wife for Isaac, the promised seed

"Now it came about after these things, that it was told Abraham, saying, 'Behold, Milcah also has borne children to your brother Nahor: Uz his firstborn and Buz his brother and Kemuel

the father of Aram and Chesed and Hazo and Pildash and Jidlaph and Bethuel.' Bethuel became the father of Rebekah; these eight Milcah bore to Nahor, Abraham's brother. His concubine, whose name was Reumah, also bore Tebah and Gaham and Tahash and Maacah" **(22:20-24).**

After the event of offering Isaac as a burnt offering, Abraham heard the news that his brother Nahor had begotten children.

If you read the preceding passage, it appears it is just saying Abraham's brother Nahor had 8 children. But through this record we can see God was leading Abraham and Isaac, the promised seed, in His precise plan. What does this mean?

In Genesis 24:3-4, we see Abraham sent his old servant, who was taking care of all his possessions, to his country and to his relatives. It was because God's chosen people Israel could never be formed through a Gentile woman. The old servant of Abraham by God's guidance met Rebekah, daughter of Bethuel, the son of Milcah, whom she bore to Nahor.

Rebekah's grandfather Nahor is Abraham's brother. And her grandmother Milcah is daughter of Haran, another brother of Abraham. So, Rebekah was a genuine descent of Abraham's family. To give a proper wife to Isaac who is the promised seed, God caused the bloodline of Abraham to be purely preserved.

God let Abraham hear the news of his brother, so that he

could be moved in his heart and get a wife for Isaac. Abraham didn't look for a woman only when the time came for Isaac to get married. He was already aware of the situation, and when the right time came, he sent his old servant.

Abraham did not do any work spontaneously. In obedience to God's moving, he prepared everything in advance and patiently waited until the right moments came. Even for the marriage of Isaac, he chose the most appropriate moment that God let him feel in his heart.

Isaac took Rebekah as his wife when he was 40 years old (Genesis 25:20). Abraham could have hurriedly gotten a wife for Isaac if he had used men's thoughts and wanted to get a wife for his son as soon as possible, so that he would have a grandchild as quickly as possible. But if he did these things in a hurry, he could have made a mistake by choosing a woman whom God didn't really want.

But Abraham didn't try to accomplish anything with human thoughts. He waited for the right time through the moving of God, and when the time came and his heart was moved by God, he selected a woman from among his relatives. Abraham always sought the will of God.

In Addition 6

The Distinction between Subordination, Obedience and Submission

What is the biggest reason Abraham was able to become the Father of Faith and the friend of God? It was because he showed his acts of obedience by believing in God who could revive the dead.

The Bible puts so much emphasis on obedience that it even says obedience is better than sacrifice. But even though the act of obedience might look the same, there are different levels of obedience depending on the heart of the one who is obeying. These levels are 'subordination', 'obedience', and 'submission'.

Subordination, Obedience, and Submission between Parents and Children

Although they don't really want to obey from the heart,

there are people who obey their parents because it's a child's duty. We can say their heart is relatively good. But if you don't obey willingly it's not true 'obedience'. It is 'subordination'.

Those children who have more of good heart obey their parents so as not to break their hearts. Even though the parents ask them to do something difficult for them to understand, they just listen to them completely and comply with their love for them. This way, they make their parents comfortable. This is obedience.

There is a higher level of obedience. It is 'submission'. Submission is to obey with an understanding of the intention and will of the one who is giving the order. When parents tell their children to do something, the children understand the parents' intention and obey them, so they can even accomplish more than what they have been told. How happy would the parents be if they have such children?

Obedience and Submission of Abraham

If God told him anything, Abraham unconditionally and immediately obeyed without giving rise to his own thoughts, even though it was something he couldn't really understand.

In Genesis 12:1, God told him, *"Go forth from your country, and from your relatives and from your father's house, to the land which I will show you."* He didn't even know where to go, and yet he just left the land of his livelihood, his family and his relatives, and set off to a strange place.

At that time, he didn't really understand the deep heart of God contained in the command given to him. He just believed God must have a good reason to give him such a command. It was with this belief he just obeyed.

The event of offering Isaac as a burnt offering in Genesis chapter 22 was more than just obedience. After he left his country in obedience to God's word and as he went through many kinds of trials, his faith in and love for God increased. And, to that same extent he could clearly understand the heart and will of God. So when God told him to offer his son Isaac as a burnt offering, he did not give any excuses but completely submitted to God.

If he had had just an inkling of human thought, Abraham couldn't have obeyed such a command as giving his only son as a burnt offering. But he didn't just believe it was in the good will of God, but he had pictured in his mind the result of his obedience. Namely, even if he had given Isaac as a burnt offering, God would have brought him back from the dead to fulfill His will through him. He understood this and completely submitted to God's will.

I have not had any illness during my entire life,
I have not had any hardship in my life.

I give You thanks
For there was no hardship or suffering
In my body or in any other aspect.
And I give thanks
For now I see the providence of God
That I will be at the bosom of the Father
After I breathe my last.

Father,
I give You thanks that I am filled with
Thanksgiving, joy and delight facing my death.

And now,
Everything is in accordance with Your providence.
Father,
Even though I lay down all these physical things
I believe that all Your plans
Will be fulfilled completely
In the providence of the Father.
And I believe that Your providence through this son
Will be completely fulfilled.

Part 3

Love and Blessings

Happiness of Having Become a Friend of God

Part 3

Abraham's journey of faith was in God's perfect love.

He followed God's will in all things, thereby receiving all kinds of blessings that a man can enjoy, including the blessing of children, health, rejuvenation, and wealth.

He loved God to the utmost degree, and he was loved by God to the same degree!

He became a shining fruit in the history of human cultivation, and he enjoys honor and glory forever in New Jerusalem, where God's throne is located.

Chapter 12

Sarah's Death and the Cave of Machpelah

- Abraham mourns his wife Sarah's death
- Walking the right way
- Declining the offer, understanding man's heart
- Buying the cave of Machpelah for funeral

1. Abraham mourns his wife Sarah's death

"Now Sarah lived one hundred and twenty-seven years; these were the years of the life of Sarah. Sarah died in Kiriath-arba (that is, Hebron) in the land of Canaan; and Abraham went in to mourn for Sarah and to weep for her. Then Abraham rose from before his dead, and spoke to the sons of Heth, saying, 'I am a stranger and a sojourner among you; give me a burial site among you that I may bury my dead out of my sight'" **(23:1-4).**

Sarah died at the age of 127 at Hebron, in Canaan. Her life was relatively shorter compared to Abraham who lived for 175 years. Being the wife of Abraham, the Father of Faith, she should have had the kind of faith that would at least come close to that of Abraham. But she still had fleshly thoughts. She was not able to cast away evil from her heart. Even though she had seen and heard a lot of things being near Abraham, she couldn't match the spiritual level of Abraham.

That does not mean, however, Abraham did not love Sarah. Of course he loved her and he wanted her to go into a good dwelling place together with him. But the result was not what he had hoped it would be.

Abraham had clear communication with God, and he knew about the afterlife very well. He knew there would be the judgment. He knew about Heaven and Hell and which dwelling place Sarah would go to with her level of faith. For this reason Abraham couldn't help himself from mourning over Sarah's death.

She had been with him for a long time and had spent the good times and bad together. She was his wife and the mother of Isaac the promised seed. Abraham wanted her to dwell in eternal glory together with him. But the result was not even close to what he hoped, and Abraham had to mourn. Then, which dwelling place in Heaven did Sarah go to after her death?

When God gave His word about Isaac, the promised seed, she couldn't believe it and laughed about it. She had seen many works of God and experienced the living God through Abraham, and yet she couldn't believe from her heart.

She couldn't unconditionally say 'Amen' to God's word. She had fleshly thoughts, and she would disobey if God's word did not agree with her thoughts. That is why Abraham couldn't tell her anything when he was going to offer Isaac as a burnt offering. It was absolutely certain that she would oppose the idea even though Abraham said it was God's will.

Also, rather than considering Isaac as the promised seed given by God, she just considered him a son whom she had late in age. She could have never agreed to offer Isaac as a burnt offering, even if she had received the command of God directly. This is, after all, because she had evil in her heart.

We can see this just by considering the way she treated Hagar and Ishmael. She had envy, jealousy, and self-seeking. She hated them and she did not like what they did. She just wanted to do everything when and as she wanted, without giving any thought about how her actions could affect others.

Of course, as this was in the times of the Old Testament, they didn't have the help of the Holy Spirit dwelling in their hearts. They could not circumcise their hearts by their own strength. By seeing the way Abraham treated Abimelech, king of Gerar, and other peoples around him she still knew that one must not misuse his power and authority but understand and accept others.

She misused the authority she had and even after a long time had passed she still kept her evil in her heart. Even though she had Abraham as such an excellent example of faith right next to her, her heart and actions didn't change. So, which dwelling place in Heaven could she go to?

Luke 12:47-48 says, *"And that slave who knew his master's will and did not get ready or act in accord with his will, will receive many lashes, but the one who did not know it, and committed deeds worthy of a flogging, will receive but few. From everyone who has been given much, much will be required; and to whom they entrusted much, of him they will ask all the more."*

Sarah certainly knew the will of God but did not practice it. She had received many things from God but she did not really give anything back to God. Although she lived in the Old Testament era, she had all the good circumstances. And yet she dwelt in flesh, and her heart and acts did not change. She was saved, but she was not qualified to go to a higher place than Paradise.

Heaven is categorized into Paradise, the lowest level of dwelling places, the First Kingdom of Heaven, the Second Kingdom of Heaven, the Third Kingdom of Heaven, and the most beautiful and glorious place, New Jerusalem.

Which of the dwelling places each one will inherit depends on the measure of each one's faith. They will receive the right to go into one of the above places depending on the extent to which they struggled and cast away sins to change their heart into the heart of truth.

Paradise is a place for those who barely received salvation. It is the lowest-level dwelling place in Heaven, and the residents there do not receive any heavenly reward. And yet, it is such a beautiful and happy place that cannot be compared with this earth. As you go up to the First Kingdom of Heaven, Second Kingdom of Heaven, and the Third Kingdom of Heaven, you will receive bigger and more beautiful houses, various crowns, and rewards.

The city of New Jerusalem is the most beautiful dwelling place in Heaven. It's a place for those who have the faith to please God and who obey Him understanding His heart and will. Personal houses in the city are as grand as big castles. They are built and decorated magnificently with pure gold and various precious stones.

There, God will reward them for everything that they wanted to do or wanted to have, but had given up for the Lord on this earth. Also, they will be envied and worshiped by heavenly host and angels and all residents of Heaven, living a happy life eternally.

Abraham is the Father of Faith, and Sarah was his wife. And the fact that she was barely saved and went to only Paradise is astonishing and shocking enough. But as we read the Bible, we can understand why she couldn't go to any higher place than Paradise. God's judgment is carried out as it is written in the Bible.

She didn't have any undeserved privilege just because she was the wife of Abraham or the mother of Isaac, the promised seed. But rather, being the wife of Abraham, it's a shame that her faith was at the lowest level.

Considering the thorough and vast knowledge of the life to come that Abraham understood, how well do you suppose that he would have taught her about those many things? He must have let her know the will of God with a great deal of teachings and advice. But Sarah couldn't keep all those things in her mind. And after all, through her death she broke Abraham's heart severely.

Abraham wanted to buy a piece of land for the burial ground of his wife Sarah, within the area they had settled. He went to the sons of Heth and said, *"I am a stranger and a sojourner among you; give me a burial site among you that I may bury my dead out of my sight."*

Of course, Abraham knew the sons of Heth wouldn't dare mistreat him, and that he could even demand what he wanted with his power, if he wanted to. He could have mentioned what he wanted from the beginning, but he first humbled himself saying he was a stranger and a sojourner.

Abraham lived among the Gentiles but he always had peace

with everybody. It's because those people feared God who was with him, and he also had strong power. Even a king couldn't deal with him lightly.

However, that didn't mean Abraham lifted himself up or looked down on others. Just by seeing the process of getting the burial site for Sarah, we can see Abraham was accurate in every matter and that he always walked the right way.

2. Walking the right way

> *"The sons of Heth answered Abraham, saying to him, 'Hear us, my lord, you are a mighty prince among us; bury your dead in the choicest of our graves; none of us will refuse you his grave for burying your dead.' So Abraham rose and bowed to the people of the land, the sons of Heth. And he spoke with them, saying, 'If it is your wish for me to bury my dead out of my sight, hear me, and approach Ephron the son of Zohar for me, that he may give me the cave of Machpelah which he owns, which is at the end of his field; for the full price let him give it to me in your presence for a burial site'"* **(23:5-9).**

Abraham made a humble request, and the sons of Heth replied, *"Hear us, my lord, you are a mighty prince among us; bury your dead in the choicest of our graves; none of us will refuse you his grave for burying your dead."*

They called Abraham 'my lord' and said he could take any grave he wanted. From this we can infer what they thought about Abraham. Abraham had such great power and authority that the sons of Heth would have to comply if he demanded a certain grave.

And yet, Abraham showed humbleness and proper manners by bowing to the people. Furthermore, even though they said they would freely give what he wanted, he said he would pay the correct price.

Abraham always wanted to follow the right way. He did not want to serve his own interests even when he was interacting with those who were lower than him. That is why he bowed to the sons of Heth politely, even though he was paying a handsome amount of money to buy the grave for his wife.

Generally, if they have more power and authority than others, people easily give orders and try to do things their own way. Especially, those who are arrogant will try to lift themselves up even higher when others acknowledge them. But it was not so with Abraham.

With the power and authority he had, he could get anything he desired. However, he did not have any desire to seek his own benefits, to covet others' belongings, or to look down upon others. Even though it cost him time and money, he just walked the right and just way, and he tried to gain the heart of others.

On the one hand, his words and attitudes came from his humility. On the other hand, they came from his wisdom. He knew the heart of fleshly people very well. Although they were saying they would give the grave to him, they could change their mind any time later. Therefore, he wanted to pay the right price and buy the grave so that there wouldn't be any possibility of conflict.

3. Declining the offer, understanding man's heart

"Now Ephron was sitting among the sons of Heth; and Ephron the Hittite answered Abraham in the hearing of the sons of Heth; even of all who went in at the gate of his city, saying, 'No, my lord, hear me; I give you the field, and I give you the cave that is in it. In the presence of the sons of my people I give it to you; bury your dead.' And Abraham bowed before the people of the land. He spoke to Ephron in the hearing of the people of the land, saying, 'If you will only please listen to me; I will give the price of the field, accept it from me that I may bury my dead there.' Then Ephron answered Abraham, saying to him, "My lord, listen to me; a piece of land worth four hundred shekels of silver, what is that between me and you? So bury your dead" **(Genesis 23:10-15).**

Abraham wanted to get the cave in a field that belonged to a person named Ephron. For the official notarization at that time, they made commercial deals at the city gate where many people were moving about. Ephron publicly said, while all the people who were coming in through the city gate could hear, that he would give Abraham any land Abraham wanted: *"No, my lord, hear me; I give you the field, and I give you the cave that is in it. In the presence of the sons of my people I give it to you; bury your dead."*

Ephron also called Abraham 'my lord'. Ephron also knew what kind of person Abraham was, and he was a lowly being compared to Abraham. Ephron publicly said he would give the land that Abraham wanted. This may sound like he would give the land for free and just serve Abraham.

But Abraham said in the hearing of the people, *"If you will only please listen to me; I will give the price of the field, accept it from me that I may bury my dead there."* Because he knew the hearts of men, he said he would pay the right price and buy the land.

What if Ephron really wanted to give Abraham the land as gift? He would have once again asked Abraham to accept his free gift. Here, the following verses tell us why Abraham wanted to refuse Ephron's offer and pay the price for the land.

Ephron replied to Abraham saying, *"My lord, listen to me;*

a piece of land worth four hundred shekels of silver, what is that between me and you? So bury your dead." Ephron initially had said he would give the land, but now he subtly mentioned the price of the land upon hearing Abraham's intention to buy the land.

He said, *"What is that between me and you?"* but in his heart, he wanted to receive the price. His inner heart was revealed by exchanging the conversation a couple of times.

Knowing this very well, how could Abraham just accept the land? If he did, there could be problems later. The sons of Ephron later could have asked the land back saying it was their father's. For this reason, Abraham paid the right price and bought the land so that there wouldn't be any problem with the right of possession.

4. Buying the cave of Machpelah for funeral

"Abraham listened to Ephron; and Abraham weighed out for Ephron the silver which he had named in the hearing of the sons of Heth, four hundred shekels of silver, commercial standard. So Ephron's field, which was in Machpelah, which faced Mamre, the field and cave which was in it, and all the trees which were in the field, that were within all the confines of its border, were deeded over to Abraham for a possession in the presence of the

sons of Heth, before all who went in at the gate of his city. After this, Abraham buried Sarah his wife in the cave of the field at Machpelah facing Mamre (that is, Hebron) in the land of Canaan. So the field and the cave that is in it, were deeded over to Abraham for a burial site by the sons of Heth" **(Genesis 23:16-20).**

Abraham gave 400 shekels of silver to Ephron as the price for the land. It is not easy to convert this amount into today's worth. But one shekel at that time was equivalent to four day's wages for ordinary labors.

If we suppose one day's wage is 100 US dollars today, one shekel is equivalent to 400 dollars. Therefore, the 400 shekels of silver is about 160,000 dollars.

Abraham made it public and official that the field, which was in Machpelah, which faced Mamre, the field and cave which was in it, and all the trees which were in the field, that were within all the confines of its border, were deeded over to him. This cave later became the grave not only for Sarah but also for Abraham, Isaac, Isaac's wife Rebekah, Jacob and his wife Leah.

Abraham dealt with all the matters through his wisdom of goodness that he never gave any room for conflicts. If you have wisdom of goodness, you can make even evil people lower their heads, and you can accomplish the kingdom of God more greatly. In order to receive this wisdom of goodness, you first have to have a generous heart to be able to give out your possessions. You have to act in an honest way without having selfish or ulterior motives.

Chapter 13

Abraham's Old Servant and Isaac's Wife, Rebekah

The old servant sets off to look for the wife for Isaac

Making an oath with trust in his master Abraham

Meeting Rebekah by the guidance of God

Telling his story in Rebekah's house

Isaac and Rebekah to be married

Isaac takes Rebekah as his wife

1. The old servant sets off to look for the wife for Isaac

"Now Abraham was old, advanced in age; and the LORD had blessed Abraham in every way. Abraham said to his servant, the oldest of his household, who had charge of all that he owned, 'Please place your hand under my thigh, and I will make you swear by the LORD, the God of heaven and the God of earth, that you shall not take a wife for my son from the daughters of the Canaanites, among whom I live, but you will go to my country and to my relatives, and take a wife for my son Isaac'" (24:1-4).

3 John 1:2 says, *"Beloved, I pray that in all respects you may prosper and be in good health, just as your soul prospers."* Abraham's life is the living testimony of this verse.

After Abraham passed the test of giving his only son, Isaac, as a burnt offering, there were only overflowing blessings in his life. Abraham was old, but his body was not weak. He rather became healthier and begot six more children.

Also, as the Bible says, *"the LORD had blessed Abraham in every way,"* he prospered in all things. He was not just rich but he also had great authority. Because God Himself intervened and opened the ways for him, whatever he harbored in his heart was done for him. There was nothing that hindered or stopped him.

Other than all those blessings Abraham received, he also had a person whom he could trust and to whom he could entrust anything. He had an old servant who managed all Abraham's possessions. Abraham's wealth was enormous, and thus, the fact that this old servant was in charge of it proves he was very trustworthy, faithful, and honest.

Saying he was an old servant doesn't only mean his advanced age. It also means he had been with Abraham in all the good times and bad. He also experienced the power of God along with his master Abraham. Furthermore, from the fact that he had been with Abraham for a long time, we can understand he served his master and loved him from his heart.

Abraham chose this servant who had faith in God and whom he could trust to give him the duty of finding the wife for Isaac. Isaac was the seed of God's promise, and the kind of wife Isaac would take could influence many things. Thus, it was a very important task.

The roles as the wife and mother were so important that Abraham was very careful when he was trying to find his daughter-in-law. So, he did not use any fleshly thoughts or men's ways, but committed everything into God's hands.

Abraham made this old servant place his hand under his thigh. Thigh is a very important part of the body, for it supports the weight of the whole body. In a spiritual sense, thigh symbolizes uprightness, and that God's promise never changes and He fulfills everything.

Therefore, when Abraham made the old servant place his hand under his thigh, it meant the relationship between Abraham and the servant was very strong. In a spiritual sense, it represents God's promise to give countless descendants through Isaac would certainly be fulfilled.

After making the old servant place his hand under his thigh, Abraham said, *"I will make you swear by the LORD, the God of heaven and the God of earth."* It was that Abraham was asking God to fulfill His promise without any hindrances. As required, this old servant was used as an instrument to fulfill this grand promise.

God guided this old servant into a prosperous way considering Abraham. Because this old servant understood this fact very well, he only relied on the God of his master Abraham in his duty to find a wife for Isaac. He did not use any of his experience or wisdom. He was very well aware that he was only a 'runner' doing his master's work.

When Abraham asked this old servant to find a wife for Isaac, he gave him one condition. It was that he had to go to Abraham's home country and to his people, and not bring any woman from the Canaanites. Isaac was the promised seed, but if he took a Gentile woman as his wife, the consequences would be devastating. Abraham understood this fact very well. Above all, because he knew what God's will was, he prohibited his old servant from bringing any Gentile woman as Isaac's wife..

At that time, Abraham was a very well-known figure, and his wealth and power were also significant. Naturally, there were many people who wanted to be his allies, and probably there would have been many women who would offer many things. But because it was made certain he couldn't bring any Gentile woman, he set out for the home country of his master.

Now, why wouldn't Abraham search for Isaac's wife himself? Wouldn't it have been better if he brought Isaac with him so that he could choose a woman for himself?

If Abraham went out to find Isaac's wife accompanied by many servants and revealing his wealth and power, probably many women would have wanted to be Isaac's wife. Most people consider the outward conditions and appearances, and are drawn to them.

Knowing this fact very well, he sent out an old servant

who didn't have any fancy outward appearance, so that there wouldn't be any women who wanted to become Isaac's wife just for his wealth. And the old servants obeyed his master's will completely.

2. Making an oath with trust in his master Abraham

> *"The servant said to him, 'Suppose the woman is not willing to follow me to this land; should I take your son back to the land from where you came?' Then Abraham said to him, 'Beware that you do not take my son back there! The LORD, the God of heaven, who took me from my father's house and from the land of my birth, and who spoke to me and who swore to me, saying, "To your descendants I will give this land," He will send His angel before you, and you will take a wife for my son from there. But if the woman is not willing to follow you, then you will be free from this my oath; only do not take my son back there." So the servant placed his hand under the thigh of Abraham his master, and swore to him concerning this matter'"* **(24:5-9).**

When asked to bring the wife for Isaac, the old servant asked Abraham a question. He wanted to know whether he should take Isaac to where the woman was, if the woman whom he would choose among relatives of Abraham wouldn't come to the land of Canaan.

The old servant was going in obedience to the word of his master, but at one corner of his heart he was wondering which woman would leave all her family and country and come with him just by hearing his words. He was not bringing the groom or any other symbol with him, so he was a bit worried that people might not believe his words.

That doesn't mean we can say this old servant was using his fleshly thoughts. If he was, he would have wanted to take Isaac with him or asked for a symbol that could confirm his words from the start.

He tried his best in his level of faith, and about what was beyond his faith, he honestly asked for the will of the master so that he could fulfill it. Rather than saying 'yes' in front of the master and then doing the work at his discretion later with his fleshly thoughts, it was much better to ask the master's will right from the beginning.

To this question of the old servant, Abraham firmly answered, *"Beware that you do not take my son back there!"* He said God would send an angel before him. Abraham was asking the servant to rely on God alone and not use any human thoughts. Abraham had that kind of faith.

God wouldn't work in finding Isaac's wife because of the old servant. The old servant was just doing the job on behalf of

Abraham, for the fulfillment of the promise of God.

Thus, the faith of the old servant was important, but his trust in his master and prophet Abraham was more important. Even for the things that couldn't be done with his faith and power, God could make it possible if he trusted his master and obeyed him.

Abraham continued to say, *"But if the woman is not willing to follow you, then you will be free from this my oath."* What would happen if the woman the old servant had chosen was not willing to follow him?

Does that mean God does not guarantee Abraham, and His promise was broken? Of course not! More precisely, it can never mean that. There won't be any occasion where the woman wouldn't be willing to follow him or the oath would be broken.

Abraham was not making any negative remarks. He said what he had said with sure faith that God would certainly fulfill His promise. That is why he could say, *"...only do not take my son back there."* It means the woman chosen, in all certainty, would follow the servant without fail.

Now the old servant placed his hand under Abraham's thigh and made an oath. This means he did not have any more questions or any doubts but he accepted all his master's words with 'Amen'. He asked a question to clear his doubts, but when his master made a profession of faith, he accepted it with faith, and not using his fleshly thoughts any more.

3. Meeting Rebekah by the guidance of God

"Then the servant took ten camels from the camels of his master, and set out with a variety of good things of his master's in his hand; and he arose and went to Mesopotamia, to the city of Nahor. He made the camels kneel down outside the city by the well of water at evening time, the time when women go out to draw water. He said, 'O LORD, the God of my master Abraham, please grant me success today, and show lovingkindness to my master Abraham. Behold, I am standing by the spring, and the daughters of the men of the city are coming out to draw water; now may it be that the girl to whom I say, "Please let down your jar so that I may drink," and who answers, "Drink, and I will water your camels also" may she be the one whom You have appointed for Your servant Isaac; and by this I will know that You have shown lovingkindness to my master.' Before he had finished speaking, behold, Rebekah who was born to Bethuel the son of Milcah, the wife of Abraham's brother Nahor, came out with her jar on her shoulder. The girl was very beautiful, a virgin, and no man had had relations with her; and she went down to the spring and filled her jar and came up. Then the servant ran to meet her, and

said, 'Please let me drink a little water from your jar.' She said, 'Drink, my lord'; and she quickly lowered her jar to her hand, and gave him a drink. Now when she had finished giving him a drink, she said, 'I will draw also for your camels until they have finished drinking.' So she quickly emptied her jar into the trough, and ran back to the well to draw, and she drew for all his camels. Meanwhile, the man was gazing at her in silence, to know whether the LORD had made his journey successful or not. When the camels had finished drinking, the man took a gold ring weighing a half-shekel and two bracelets for her wrists weighing ten shekels in gold, and said, 'Whose daughter are you? Please tell me, is there room for us to lodge in your father's house?' She said to him, 'I am the daughter of Bethuel, the son of Milcah, whom she bore to Nahor.' Again she said to him, 'We have plenty of both straw and feed, and room to lodge in.' Then the man bowed low and worshiped the LORD. He said, 'Blessed be the LORD, the God of my master Abraham, who has not forsaken His lovingkindness and His truth toward my master; as for me, the LORD has guided me in the way to the house of my master's brothers'" (24:10-27).

Finally, the old servant set out with ten camels from the camels of his master and a variety of good things of his master's in his hand. They were not for himself or for his gain, but he was to give them to the woman he was going to meet as gift that would deliver his master's heart.

These gifts were later delivered to Rebekah and her family. Silver and gold and jewelry were given to Rebekah, and other gifts were also given to her brother and mother. It was not a way to win their favor. If it were so, he would have shown the gifts first. But the gifts were given only after Rebekah decided to become Isaac's wife. We can easily see that these gifts were given to deliver the heart of his master to the woman and her family.

The old servant went to Mesopotamia, to the city of Nahor. It's not that he knew where he was supposed to go. It was only later that he found out it was a city where Abraham's brother was living, and said, *"Blessed be the LORD, the God of my master Abraham."*

He reached outside the city by the well of water at evening time, the exact time when women came out to draw water. It was also delicate guidance of God. This way, he could meet the woman prepared by God as quickly as possible.

Here, the servant prayed to God so that He would make everything go well, for his master Abraham's sake. He said, *"O LORD, the God of my master Abraham, please grant me success today, and show lovingkindness to my master Abraham."*

He made sure that the guidance of God in his job was God's grace given to his master Abraham. He did not have any intention to take the credit for himself saying, "I found the woman with my effort." He professed that his task would be fulfilled by the grace of God because of his master Abraham.

Why would God not answer this servant's prayer which was offered without any selfish motive! The old servant met a woman named Rebekah at that place. Now, how did the old servant recognize this woman to be the one prepared by God? Committing everything into God's hands, the old servant prayed as follows:

> *"Behold, I am standing by the spring, and the daughters of the men of the city are coming out to draw water; now may it be that the girl to whom I say, 'Please let down your jar so that I may drink,' and who answers, 'Drink, and I will water your camels also' may she be the one whom You have appointed for Your servant Isaac; and by this I will know that You have shown lovingkindness to my master."*

The servant asked God for a clear sign. God heard his prayer and granted him what he asked as he asked. Even before the prayer was over, a woman approached the well of water with her jar on her shoulder. When he asked for some water, she didn't only help him drink but also watered the camels, too.

She acted almost as though she had heard the prayer of the old servant. What kind of emotion do you think the servant had at that moment? He must have been moved giving thanks to God who heard his prayer for his master's sake. But the old servant was very careful. He did not just draw the conclusion that she was the one he was looking for, but he wanted to reconfirm that it was God's guidance.

The servant gave a gold ring and two gold bracelets for her wrists, and said, *"Whose daughter are you? Please tell me, is there room for us to lodge in your father's house?"* She said to him, *"I am the daughter of Bethuel, the son of Milcah, whom she bore to Nahor."*

Before this old servant set out his journey, he heard about Abraham's family and relatives. Abraham usually kept track of his relatives living in his home country, and told his servant what he knew about them. For this reason, the servant was able to realize he was guided to the right place the moment he heard the names Nahor, Milcah, and Bethuel.

He was reassured that God was in control and it was the result of God's guidance. Before this work of God, the servant bowed his head and worshiped God to give Him glory.

4. Telling his story in Rebekah's house

"Then the girl ran and told her mother's household about these things. Now Rebekah had a brother whose name was Laban; and Laban ran outside to the man at the spring. When he saw the ring and the bracelets on his sister's wrists, and when he heard the words of Rebekah his sister, saying, 'This is what the man said to me,' he went to the man; and behold, he was standing by the camels at the spring. And he said, 'Come in, blessed of the LORD! Why do you stand outside since I have prepared the house, and a place for the camels?' So the man entered the house. Then Laban unloaded the camels, and he gave straw and feed to the camels, and water to wash his feet and the feet of the men who were with him. But when food was set before him to eat, he said, 'I will not eat until I have told my business.' And he said, 'Speak on.' So he said, 'I am Abraham's servant. The LORD has greatly blessed my master, so that he has become rich; and He has given him flocks and herds, and silver and gold, and servants and maids, and camels and donkeys. Now Sarah my master's wife bore a son to my master in her old age, and he has given him all that he has. My master made me swear, saying, "You shall not take a wife for my son from the daughters of the Canaanites, in whose land I live; but you shall go to my father's house and to my relatives, and take a wife for my son"'" (24:28-38).

"Then I asked her, and said, 'Whose daughter are you?' And she said, 'The daughter of Bethuel, Nahor's son, whom Milcah bore to him'; and I put the ring on her nose, and the bracelets on her wrists. And I bowed low and worshiped the LORD, and blessed the LORD, the God of my master Abraham, who had guided me in the right way to take the daughter of my master's kinsman for his son. So now if you are going to deal kindly and truly with my master, tell me; and if not, let me know, that I may turn to the right hand or the left" (24:47-48).

In the viewpoint of Rebekah, she couldn't understand the significance of meeting with the old servant. When she went out to the well to draw water, a man asked for water and she just let him drink. His camels also looked tired, so she gave them water, too. The man then asked her whose daughter she was, so she just told him the names of her grandfather, grandmother, and father.

But he became so happy and offered a thanksgiving prayer to God saying God guided him to the house of the brother of his master Abraham. Rebekah went home and explained what happened.

Hearing the words of Rebekah, her brother Laban went out to the well to receive the old servant into his house. Laban unloaded the camels, and he gave straw and feed to the camels, and water to wash the old servant's feet and the feet of the men who were with him. But when food was set before him to eat, he explained why he made the visit.

He introduced his master Abraham and explained why he came to this place, and how he met Rebekah. He explained, at the well of water, that he had prayed he would choose the woman, if the woman would give him water and also to the camels when he asked for water.

And Rebekah did exactly as he had prayed. He continued to explain. When he asked her whose daughter she was, she answered, "The daughter of Bethuel, Nahor's son, whom Milcah bore to him." He knew she was a relative of Abraham and was convinced that she was the bride for Isaac whom God had prepared. After explaining all these, he asked Rebekah's father Bethuel and her brother Laban to decide whether or not they were going to send her away to be married to Isaac.

5. Isaac and Rebekah to be married

"Then Laban and Bethuel replied, 'The matter comes from the LORD; so we cannot speak to you bad or good. Here is Rebekah before you, take her and go, and let her be the wife of your master's son, as the LORD has spoken.' When Abraham's servant heard their words, he bowed himself to the ground before the LORD. The servant brought out articles of silver and articles of gold, and

garments, and gave them to Rebekah; he also gave precious things to her brother and to her mother. Then he and the men who were with him ate and drank and spent the night. When they arose in the morning, he said, 'Send me away to my master.' But her brother and her mother said, 'Let the girl stay with us a few days, say ten; afterward she may go.' He said to them, 'Do not delay me, since the LORD has prospered my way. Send me away that I may go to my master.' And they said, 'We will call the girl and consult her wishes.' Then they called Rebekah and said to her, 'Will you go with this man?' And she said, 'I will go.' Thus they sent away their sister Rebekah and her nurse with Abraham's servant and his men. They blessed Rebekah and said to her, 'May you, our sister, become thousands of ten thousands, and may your descendants possess the gate of those who hate them'" **(24:50-60).**

After hearing everything, Bethuel and Laban replied, *"The matter comes from the LORD; so we cannot speak to you bad or good. Here is Rebekah before you, take her and go, and let her be the wife of your master's son, as the LORD has spoken."* Things were progressing without any hindrance.

First, the old servant bowed himself to the ground before the LORD. Then, he brought out articles of silver and articles of gold, and garments, and gave them to Rebekah, and he also gave precious things to her brother and to her mother. He gave these presents to Rebekah and her family only after they had reached an agreement, so that he could actually convey the heart of his master.

The servant stayed the night there. Right after he got up next morning, he said he wanted to hurry back to his master with Rebekah. Surprised, Rebekah's mother and her brother Laban said they wanted to spend at least ten days with her. But the servant insisted he had to leave.

They finally agreed to decide what to do after asking Rebekah what she wanted. She said she wanted to listen to the servant. God did not just move the heart of the old servant but also those of Rebekah and her family. Everything was done so naturally that it looked as if it was all a well-thought-out plan.

If Rebekah just thought about her love for the family members, she could have wished to stay with her family a little longer. But as God moved her heart for Abraham's sake, she just followed the old servant's words. Finally, as Rebekah was leaving to become Isaac's wife, Laban and her mother blessed her saying, *"May you, our sister, become thousands of ten thousands, and may your descendants possess the gate of those who hate them."*

This blessing was in line with the promise of God given to Abraham saying, *"your seed shall possess the gate of their enemies"* (Genesis 22:17), and this blessing was fulfilled through Jesus who was born among the Israelites.

6. Isaac takes Rebekah as his wife

"Then Rebekah arose with her maids, and they mounted the camels and followed the man. So the servant took Rebekah and departed. Now Isaac had come from going to Beer-lahai-roi; for he was living in the Negev. Isaac went out to meditate in the field toward evening; and he lifted up his eyes and looked, and behold, camels were coming. Rebekah lifted up her eyes, and when she saw Isaac she dismounted from the camel. She said to the servant, 'Who is that man walking in the field to meet us?' And the servant said, 'He is my master.' Then she took her veil and covered herself. The servant told Isaac all the things that he had done. Then Isaac brought her into his mother Sarah's tent, and he took Rebekah, and she became his wife, and he loved her; thus Isaac was comforted after his mother's death" **(24:61-67).**

Rebekah left behind her beloved family and hometown, and set out with the old servant for a new start.

One evening, while Isaac was meditating out in the field, he saw the camels coming. When Rebekah found out the man approaching was Isaac, she took her veil and covered her face. The servant told Isaac everything that had happened.

Isaac finally met the wife prepared by God, and brought her into his mother Sarah's tent. Rebekah, as Isaac's wife, was blessed to participate in God's promise given to Abraham, the

Father of Faith.

… In Addition 7

Abraham's Old Servant's Attitude and Heart

The Heart of the Old Servant in Asking God for a Sign

Before he met with the woman who was going to be Isaac's wife, the old servant of Abraham asked God for a specific sign. Namely, he said, if the woman would act in a certain way, he would know that she was the one prepared by God to be Isaac's wife.

This was not to test God. He neither sought any luck nor did he put up conditions before God with an ulterior motive. He prayed with a good heart and only wanted to fulfill the request of his master by God's guidance.

Hearing his prayer, God did not say he was testing Him, but rather He was touched by his heart, and He answered him. The reason why the old servant asked God for a sign was because he completely believed God would make his way prosperous for Abraham's sake.

The old servant understood God's will clearly

When the old servant witnessed his prayer being fulfilled exactly as he had prayed, he did not draw a hasty conclusion. He prayed in the spirit of God, and his prayer was answered, but he was very careful to check and reconfirm God's will. Only when he had clear sign once again did he truly understand it was God's answer, and he then gave honor and glory to God.

Here, we have to understand seeking evidence again just because God's answer is different from our thoughts and we have doubts and the old servant's trying to reconfirm God's will are two completely different cases.

Meaning of the ring and bracelets given to Rebekah

A ring usually carries the meaning of 'binding' or 'bond' but here it means 'connecting the works of God' and 'confirming and defining those works'. After all, the old servant giving the ring and bracelets to Rebekah symbolized that the task was completed. It was a kind of symbol that signified the works of

God were fulfilled.

The old servant delivers only facts to Laban

When the old servant was explaining the proceedings of the matter, he was very precise. He explained what instruction he had received from his master; how he prayed before God; and how his prayer was answered. He did not change any words that his master spoke to him nor did he interpret them at his discretion. Even about the works of God, he did not add any personal interpretations but only delivered the facts.

Because he accurately explained about the providence of God, Laban could not help but say, "The matter comes from the LORD." Only when we have a truthful heart, can we deliver words correctly and we will not change the words for our benefit.

The old servant does not try to serve his interest at all

The old servant was faithful to his duty even after he was invited into Laban's house. He said, "I will not eat until I have told my business." He wasn't thinking like, 'I am tired from the long journey, and it seems things are going very well, so I'll discuss the matter with them after I eat first.' He ate and drank only after all things were settled.

Furthermore, after staying one night there, he rushed to go back to his master right away. He didn't have any wish to take a rest there for several days or to enjoy the hospitality of Rebekah's family in full, just because he had fulfilled his duty. He only wanted to deliver the good news to his master as soon as possible. He thought about his master who must be so eagerly waiting for him.

Until the moment he completed his task and returned to his master, his mind was focused on fulfilling his duty. Because he was such a servant who could accomplish the task with the heart of the master, he was trusted by Abraham, and God could make his way prosperous.

Chapter 14

Death of Abraham, Father of Faith and His Duty

Descendants of the six sons born of Keturah
Isaac succeeds the orthodox genealogy
Abraham's death and burial

1. Descendants of the six sons born of Keturah

"Now Abraham took another wife, whose name was Keturah. She bore to him Zimran and Jokshan and Medan and Midian and Ishbak and Shuah. Jokshan became the father of Sheba and Dedan. And the sons of Dedan were Asshurim and Letushim and Leummim. The sons of Midian were Ephah and Epher and Hanoch and Abida and Eldaah. All these were the sons of Keturah" **(25:1-4).**

After Sarah died, Abraham took a second wife named Keturah. He was more than 140 years old; he had begotten Isaac at the age of 100, and he took Keturah after Isaac got married at the age of 40.

Abraham already had two sons, namely Isaac the promised seed and Ishmael born of Hagar. Here lies an important point. God said He would give Abraham a son when he was 99. Already, his body physically could not have a son. Now, he was more than 140 years old, and he begot six more sons.

It tells us that after Abraham's faith was perfected, he was rejuvenated, and he enjoyed a healthy and happy life during his last days. The six sons born of Keturah were not part of the orthodox genealogy of Abraham, but they also formed nations later and became a part of the history of human cultivation.

God made a promise when He called Abraham, saying, *"And I will make you a great nation, and I will bless you, and make your name great; and so you shall be a blessing; and I will bless those who bless you, and the one who curses you I will curse. And in you all the families of the earth will be blessed"* (Genesis 12:2-3).

As God had promised, Abraham became the Father of Faith and source of blessings. His soul was prosperous, and He received blessings of wealth, health, and children.

God formed the nation of Israel through the orthodox genealogy of Isaac and fulfilled His promise that Abraham would be the channel of blessing for all nations on the earth. It was fulfilled when Jesus came to the land of Israel as a son of David and Abraham and opened the way of salvation for all peoples.

God also provided the foundation for many nations to be formed through other sons than Isaac. Ishmael and the six sons of Keturah later formed the Arabian nations. As time passed these peoples mixed with each other. The people of Midian,

Ephah, and Sheba in Isaiah chapter 60 are all descendants of six sons of Keturah, and people of Kedar and Nebiaoth are children of Ishmael.

2. Isaac succeeds the orthodox genealogy

> *"Now Abraham gave all that he had to Isaac; but to the sons of his concubines, Abraham gave gifts while he was still living, and sent them away from his son Isaac eastward, to the land of the east"* (25:5-6).

Knowing that his end on this earth was drawing near, Abraham, according to God's will, gave all that he had to Isaac. He also gave gifts to the sons of his concubines. Furthermore, he sent them all away from his son Isaac while he was still living.

Why did Abraham do this? It was so that the providence of God that had to be fulfilled through Isaac would not be hindered in any way by the sons of concubines. Outwardly this looks like Sarah sending Ishmael away from Isaac in the past, but actually it is very different.

On the one hand, when Sarah sent Ishmael away, it was due to her fleshly thoughts thinking there might be a problem for Isaac to succeed the orthodox genealogy because of Ishmael. Also, she was worried Ishmael might harm Isaac in one way or

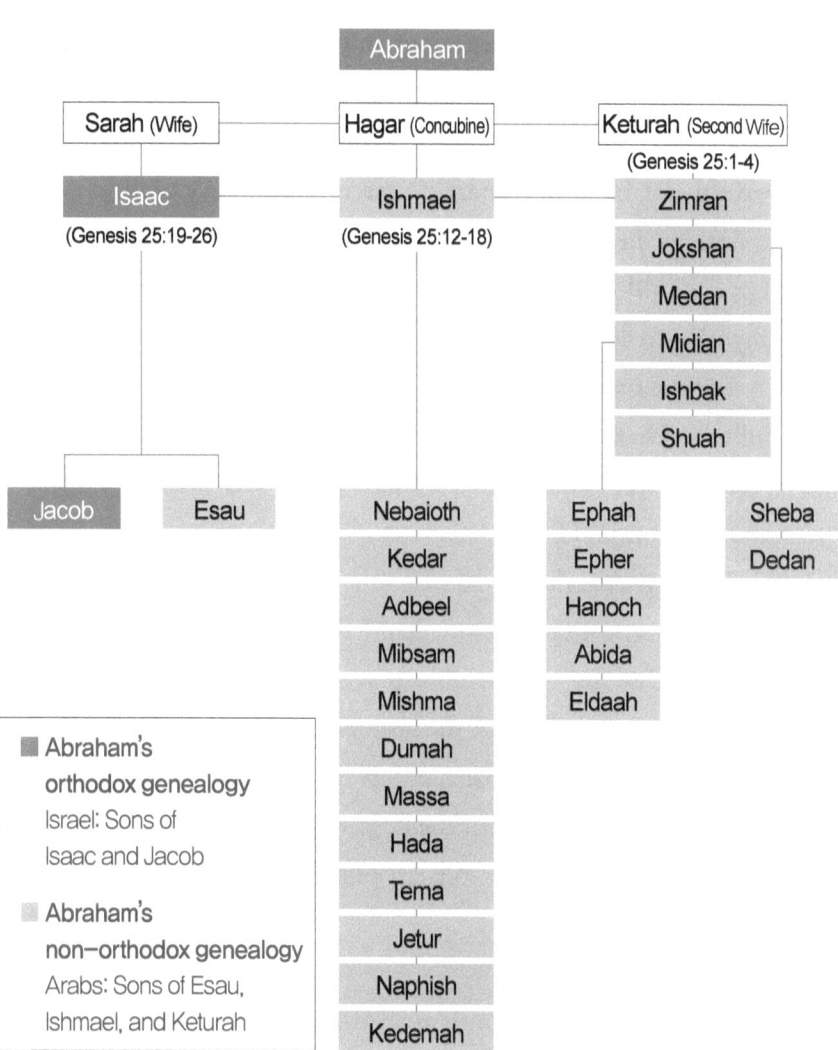

253

another.

On the other hand, when Abraham sent other sons away from Isaac towards the end of his life, it was not out of fleshly thought or worries. He knew that the nation that would succeed the orthodox genealogy in God's providence would only come through Isaac.

He also knew other sons than Isaac, the promised seed, would not be able to participate in Abraham's orthodox genealogy. In other words, the descendants of other sons than Isaac would eventually leave God and they wouldn't have anything to do with God as time passes.

For the time being, the children were still under Abraham's influence, so they revered God and lived in God's will. But after Abraham would die, eventually, they would stop revering God and depart from Him.

What if Abraham had not sent them away because of his fleshly affections toward them? Right now it might look good because they would all be together, but later, these sons' descendants might damage the orthodoxy of the descendants of Isaac. Even if the descendants of Isaac tried to keep God's ways, if they lived together with the descendants of other brothers who would depart from God, certainly they would be affected in one way or another.

Now, what is the fundamental reason God wanted to

continue the orthodox genealogy of Abraham through Isaac? It is because God wanted Abraham's heart and service to be passed on.

What if the descendants of Isaac also changed their heart and service to God because of the descendants of other sons who do not keep the laws of God? For this reason Abraham had to set apart Isaac and other sons who would depart from the orthodoxy—the ways of God. It is like spirit and flesh cannot co-exist (2 Corinthians 6:14).

Because Abraham knew God's great plan, he was not emotionally attached by his personal affection toward his children. That is why he sent his other sons away with gifts so they could become independent.

But it doesn't mean Abraham had any intention to discriminate against the other sons. It was something natural at that time to give all the possessions to the legitimate son. And, at the same time he gave some wealth to other sons also, so they could settle down and become independent.

As a matter of fact, it was not a rule that other sons had to lose the orthodoxy as Abraham's children. But it's just that God foreknew how they would change, so He moved Abraham's heart to let them go. Even though they were not the heirs to continue Abraham's genealogy, what if they kept the teachings of Abraham, and revered and served God only?

Would God have said, "You are not the chosen ones, so you can never be blessed"? Of course not! He would have opened a way of salvation for them and let them live in God's blessings. After all, the reason why they couldn't receive God's blessing was not because they were not chosen but because they were not prepared to receive blessings in their heart and actions.

God is not like a dictator who decides everything on his own and forces everyone to follow him. He gives fair opportunities to everyone and lets them choose with their freewill. However, some people do not enter into God's grace because they do not take hold of these opportunities.

3. Abraham's death and burial

> "These are all the years of Abraham's life that he lived, one hundred and seventy-five years. Abraham breathed his last and died in a ripe old age, an old man and satisfied with life; and he was gathered to his people. Then his sons Isaac and Ishmael buried him in the cave of Machpelah, in the field of Ephron the son of Zohar the Hittite, facing Mamre, the field which Abraham purchased from the sons of Heth; there Abraham was buried with Sarah his wife. It came about after the death of Abraham, that God blessed his son Isaac; and Isaac lived by Beer-lahai-roi" (25:7-11).

Abraham lived such a blessed life that he envied no one on this earth, but he also had to face the end of this life. He breathed his last at the age of 175. It is not that he died of a disease or that he became weak due to old age. His soul prospered, so he was always healthy. But it's just that Abraham had to pass the stage of physical death when the time came.

He died in peace with so much comfort. He very comfortably breathed his last because God took away all the energy from his body. He had peace until the moment of his death because he loved God to the utmost degree and was loved by God.

From the moment he was born until he was established as the Father of Faith, and eventually until the end of his life on this earth, he obeyed God in all things. For this reason he was led by God in every matter, with nothing going wrong.

Furthermore, Abraham knew when he was going to face his death. It's not that he felt he was too weak to live any longer. God moved his heart, and he could wrap up every matter in his life and faced his last moment in thanksgiving. He finished all his duties on this earth. He finished his life in such a beautiful way, thinking of the beloved Father God whom he was going to see soon.

Abraham set an example of perfect faith, which had no defect at all in the view of justice. Being worthy to be called the Father of Faith, he showed the kind of faith to completely trust and obey God. He became a shining fruit in the history of human cultivation.

How happy would you be if you have a lifelong friend with whom you can share your heart and share all your secrets? Just by thinking of such a friend, you'd be glad and feel the warmth in your heart. Abraham deeply understood the heart of God and shared his heart with Him. How did God feel about this Abraham, who was like a friend to Him?

Abraham became inexpressible comfort and joy to God the Father who had to endure so much pain for a long time during the course of human history.

Isaac and Ishmael buried their father Abraham in the cave of Machpelah where Sarah was buried. After Abraham was buried, God blessed Isaac. From this moment it was the glory days of Isaac who continued the orthodox genealogy of Abraham.

In Addition 8

Abraham entered New Jerusalem, the most beautiful heavenly dwelling place

When we go to Heaven, the dwelling place will be different according to our measure of faith. Those who have holy hearts and have been faithful in all God's household can go into New Jerusalem, where the throne of God is located.

Revelation chapter 21 talks about the city of New Jerusalem that is beautiful, clear as crystal and has the glory of God. It talks about the twelve pearl gates that have the names of the twelve tribes of Israel, the twelve foundations that have the names of the twelve apostles of the Lord, and the size of the city and the city walls.

The size and beauty of the city of New Jerusalem are beyond our imagination. There are endless arrays of buildings that are built with colorful precious stones and gold. At the center of the city is located the throne of God from which the River of the Water of Life begins. Around the throne are the houses of the patriarchs who were acknowledged by God, such as Elijah, Enoch, Abraham, Moses, and the apostle Paul, and women who loved God to the utmost degree, such as Mary Magdalene and the Virgin Mary.

Abraham's heavenly house inscribed with "My Lovely Friend"

Abraham's residence is more of a castle than a simple house. The whole castle is made of gold that has bluish light. As he is the Father of Faith, the size of the castle is very big, and overall it has a round shape. At the center is a round-shaped, golden roof. Underneath it is an inscription that says, 'My Lovely Friend'. As the gate opens, beautiful lights come out, the chirping of the pretty birds is heard, and the fragrance of the flowers can be strongly smelled.

On the walls of the home the life history of Abraham is inscribed. It feels like you are reading a beautiful poem. As you open the front door, you can see the big, wide ballroom. It has multiple numbers of chandeliers on the ceiling. The ballroom is so big and wide that the chandeliers look like twinkling stars.

In Heaven, the spiritual rank will be decided according to the extent to which one takes after God's heart. It is decided by the brightness of the light, the depth of goodness, and the size of love, and thus, nobody has any complaint. And because there is no evil mind at all, they follow the spiritual order all the time.

Even though they are in the same room, they feel the difference of spiritual level clearly if somebody is ahead of them, and respect and love for them naturally flow out from the heart. In order for us to dwell near the throne of God, above all, we have to take after the heart of God.

Abraham's duty at the Great White Throne Judgment

As we have seen in Genesis chapter 12 onward, Abraham received a calling of God and had achieved a heart as clear and beautiful as crystal. Also, with his true faith and obedience he received overflowing blessings on this earth as well. He became the source of blessings and a friend of God (James 2:23). He reached a very high place in the order in Heaven as well.

In the Great White Throne Judgment, God the Father is the judge, and the Lord and the Holy Spirit guarantee the correctness of the judgment with the standpoint of human beings. The Lord came to this earth in a human body and experienced all the things that human beings go through. The Holy Spirit knows the heart of men better than anybody.

But this is not the end of the judgment. There are more steps of confirmation. Those who are recognized of their holiness by God will assist in the Great Judgment. As for these people, they received the glory before God, and they have the perfected heavenly body already, and thus, there is no reason for them to be judged. It's just that they have the duty of assisting God in the Great Judgment.

Elijah and Enoch, who were caught up to Heaven without seeing physical death, will serve as a standard of judgment just by the fact that they are the best of the fruits of human cultivation. Abraham will assist in the Great Judgment in view of faith and Moses in view of the Law, by elaborating on about how well a particular soul being judged has kept the words of God.

Abraham's confession, as the Father of Faith

Father, You are the origin of everything. You are the completion of everything.

You are the perfection of everything. You are the ruler of everything.

I offer my praises before You, my Father, the LORD God.

I was a truly lowly being. But You made me.

You molded me and harbored me in Your heart.

You accomplished perfection in me and promised me many things.

And You kept all Your promises faithfully.

I give great glory before You, the Father God.

I was nothing,
But You, my Father, loved me and chose me,
And showed You are the living, God the Father,
And You are lifting up Your glory.

Father, I give You thanks.
I praise the Father with my lips.
My praises and glory will reach the Father completely.
Through this son, through this lowly and truly lowly man,
You fulfill Your will, the will of the LORD God.

Abraham's confession in Heaven

In all my deeds and all my heart,
Was there anything that was cultivated without the help of the Father?

I remember the promises of the Father seeing the stars in the night sky.
I remember the promises of the Father seeing the Oaktree.
I missed the Father, just by seeing an unclear shape far away.

I couldn't just miss anything that came into my eyes,
Because I was always looking for the Father's hands and Father's love.

Giving my son as a burnt offering,
I felt this was also deep love of the Father,
I shed tears touched by the heart of the Father who has trusted me.

Father, with Your love,
You always think about me, and You want to give me only blessings.
And now this love has established this son as the Father of Faith.

I have been happy in this life on this earth because of the Father.

In this generation, is there anyone who is as blessed as I am?

I give thanks to the Father,

To my beloved Father.

Abraham's confession in Heaven

Father, You are great and vast.

Father, Your glory is dazzling and it is beyond words.

Father, Your love fills the heart of this son and it overflows.

How can I speak of this joy?

How can I deliver this happiness?

My Father is great and vast.

The Author
Dr. Jaerock Lee

Dr. Jaerock Lee was born in Muan, Jeonnam Province, Republic of Korea, in 1943. While in his twenties, Dr. Lee suffered from a variety of incurable diseases for seven years and awaited death with no hope for recovery. However one day in the spring of 1974 he was led to a church by his sister, and when he knelt down to pray, the living God immediately healed him of all his diseases.

From the moment he met the living God through that wonderful experience, Dr. Lee has loved God with all his heart and sincerity, and in 1978 he was called to be a servant of God. He prayed fervently with countless fasting prayers so that he could clearly understand the will of God, wholly accomplish it and obey the Word of God. In 1982, he founded Manmin Central Church in Seoul, South Korea, and countless works of God, including miraculous healings, signs and wonders, have been taking place at his church ever since.

In 1986, Dr. Lee was ordained as a pastor at the Annual Assembly of Jesus' Sungkyul(Holiness) Church of Korea, and four years later in 1990, his sermons began to be broadcast in Australia, Russia, and the Philippines. Within a short time many more countries were being reached through the Far East Broadcasting Company, the Asia Broadcast Station, and the Washington Christian Radio System.

Three years later, in 1993, Manmin Central Church was selected as one of the "World's Top 50 Churches" by the Christian World magazine (US) and he received an Honorary Doctorate of Divinity from Christian Faith College, Florida, USA, and in 1996 he received his Ph. D. in Ministry from Kingsway Theological Seminary, Iowa, USA.

Since 1993, Dr. Lee has been spearheading world evangelization through many overseas crusades in Tanzania, Argentina, L.A., Baltimore City, Hawaii, and New York City of the USA, Uganda, Japan, Pakistan, Kenya, the Philippines, Honduras, India, Russia, Germany, Peru, Democratic Republic of the Congo, Israel and Estonia.

In 2002 he was acknowledged as a "worldwide revivalist" for his powerful ministries in various overseas crusades by major Christian newspapers in Korea. In particular was his 'New York Crusade 2006' held in Madison Square Garden, the most famous arena in the world. The event was broadcast to 220 nations, and in his 'Israel United Crusade 2009', held at the International Convention Center (ICC) in Jerusalem he boldly proclaimed Jesus Christ is the Messiah and Savior.

His sermons are broadcast to 176 nations via satellites including GCN TV and he was listed as one of the 'Top 10 Most Influential Christian Leaders' of 2009 and 2010 by the popular Russian Christian magazine *In Victory* and news agency *Christian Telegraph* for his powerful TV broadcasting ministry and overseas church-pastoring ministry.

As of February of 2017, Manmin Central Church has a congregation of more than 120,000 members. There are 11,000 branch churches worldwide including 56 domestic branch churches, and more than 103 missionaries have been commissioned to 23 countries, including the United States, Russia, Germany, Canada, Japan, China, France, India, Kenya, and many more so far.

As of the date of this publishing, Dr. Lee has written 106 books, including bestsellers *Tasting Eternal Life before Death, My Life My Faith I & II, The Message of the Cross, The Measure of Faith, Heaven I & II, Hell, Awaken Israel!,* and *The Power of God*. His works have been translated into more than 76 languages.

His Christian columns appear on *The Hankook Ilbo, The JoongAng Daily, The Chosun Ilbo, The Dong-A Ilbo, The Hankyoreh Shinmun, The Seoul Shinmun, The Kyunghyang Shinmun, The Korea Economic Daily, The Korea Herald, The Shisa News,* and *The Christian Press*.

Dr. Lee is currently leader of many missionary organizations and associations. Positions include: Chairman, The United Holiness Church of Jesus Christ; Permanent President, The World Christianity Revival Mission Association; Founder & Board Chairman, Global Christian Network (GCN); Founder & Board Chairman, World Christian Doctors Network (WCDN); and Founder & Board Chairman, Manmin International Seminary (MIS).

Other powerful books by the same author

Heaven I & II

A detailed sketch of the gorgeous living environment the heavenly citizens enjoy and beautiful description of different levels of heavenly kingdoms.

Tasting Eternal Life Before Death

A testimonial memoirs of Dr. Jaerock Lee, who was born again and saved from the valley of the shadow of death and has been leading a perfect exemplary Christian life.

Hell

An earnest message to all mankind from God, who wishes not even one soul to fall into the depths of hell! You will discover the never-before-revealed account of the cruel reality of the Lower Grave and Hell.

My Life My Faith I & II

Dr. Jaerock Lee's autobiography provides the most fragrant spiritual aroma for the readers, through his life extracted from the love of God blossomed in midst of the dark waves, cold yoke and the deepest despair.

The Measure of Faith

What kind of a dwelling place, crown and reward are prepared for you in heaven? This book provides with wisdom and guidance for you to measure your faith and cultivate the best and most mature faith.

Spirit, Soul, and Body I & II

A guidebook that gives the reader spiritual understanding of spirit, soul, and body, and helps him find what kind of 'self' he has made so that he can gain the power to defeat darkness and become a person of spirit.

Awaken, Israel

Why has God kept His eyes on Israel from the beginning of the world to this day? What kind of His providence has been prepared for Israel in the last days, who await the Messiah?

Seven Churches

The Lord's earnest messages awakening believers and churches from spiritual slumber, sent to the seven churches recorded in Revelation chapter 2 and 3, which refer to all the churches of the Lord

Footsteps of the Lord I & II

An unraveled account of secrets about the beginning of time, the origin of Jesus, and God's providence and love for allowing His only begotten Son Passion and resurrection!

The Power of God

This is a 'must-read' that serves as an essential guide by which one can possess true faith and experience the wondrous power of God

www.urimbooks.com

Professions

God clearly let me know His endless heart and will that is contained in the Bible. He also let me know the Professions that God, the Lord, and the patriarchs of faith made from their hearts.

Against Such Things There Is No Law

As they bear the fruits of the Holy Spirit, Christians gain true freedom and can check themselves as to how sanctified they are, how close they can get to God's throne, and as to how much they have cultivated the heart of the Lord.

Love: Fulfillment of the Law

Spiritual love is to love the other person with an unchanging heart not desiring anything in return; however, fleshly love changes in different situations and circumstances. This book guides readers to possess spiritual love that is precious and beautiful.

A Man Who Pursues True Blessing

Jesus' message titled "Beatitudes" helps us realize what true blessing is so that we will not only enjoy all the blessings of this world including wealth, health, fame, and authority, but possess New Jerusalem.

Lectures on the First Corinthians I & II

A 'basics' guidebook for Christian accounting and ways to resolve various life problems including lawsuits, strife, marriage, idolatry, and the spiritual gifts and for the victory in spiritual warfare.

www.urimbooks.com

www.ingramcontent.com/pod-product-compliance
Lightning Source LLC
LaVergne TN
LVHW091720070526
838199LV00050B/2475